THE EQUICENTRAL BOOK 1

MW00475126

Horse Ownership Responsible Sustainable Ethical

Jane Myers and Stuart Myers
Equiculture Publishing

Disclaimer

About this book

With horse ownership comes great responsibility; we have a responsibility to manage our horses to the best of our ability and to do this sustainably and ethically.

Horse keeping has changed dramatically in the last 30 to 40 years and there are many new challenges facing contemporary horse owners. The modern domestic horse is now much more likely to be kept for leisure purposes than for work and this can have huge implications on the health and well-being of our horses and create heavy demands on our time and resources.

We need to rethink how we keep horses today rather than carry on doing things traditionally simply because that is 'how it has always been done'. We need to look at how we can develop practices that ensure that their needs are met, without compromising their welfare, the environment and our own lifestyle.

This book brings together much of the current research and thinking on responsible, sustainable, ethical horsekeeping so that you can make informed choices when it comes to your own horse management practices. It starts by looking at the way we traditionally keep horses and how this has come about. It then discusses some contemporary issues and offers some solutions in particular a system of horsekeeping that we have developed and call **The Equicentral System.**

For many years now we have been teaching this management system to horse owners in various climates around the world, to great effect. This system has many advantages for the 'lifestyle' of your horse/s, your own lifestyle and for the wider environment - all at the same time, a true win-win situation all round.

Thank you for buying this book and please consider either leaving a review or contacting us with feedback, **stuart@equiculture.com.au.**

About the authors

Jane Myers MSc (Equine Science) is the author of several professional books about horses including the best selling book **Managing Horses on Small Properties** (published by CSIRO).

Jane has lived and breathed horses from a young age and considers herself to be very fortunate in that she has been able to spend her life riding, training and studying these amazing animals.

Stuart Myers (BSc) has a background in human behaviour and has been a horse husband for more years than he cares to remember.

Jane and Stuart are particularly interested in sustainable horsekeeping practices and issues, such as low stress horse management that also delivers environmental benefits. They present workshops to horse owners in Australia, the USA and the UK about sustainable horse and horse property management as part of their business, **Equiculture**.

Their experience is second to none when it comes to this subject as they keep up with recent advances/research and are involved in research themselves. They travel the world as part of their work and they bring this information to you via their books, online resources and website.

See the **Equiculture website www.equiculture.com.au** where you will find lots of great information about sustainable horsekeeping and please join the mailing list while you are there!

Jane and Stuart also have another website that supports their **Horse Rider's Mechanic** series of workbooks. This website is **www.horseridersmechanic.com** why not have a look?

Photo credits

All photos and diagrams by Jane Myers and Stuart Myers unless otherwise accredited. Any errors and omissions please let us know.

Contents

Chapter 4: Horse behaviour, welfare and lifestyle 41

Chapter 1: Introduction

With horse ownership comes great responsibility, we have a responsibility to manage our horses to the best of our ability and to do this *sustainably* and *ethically*.

The development of horsekeeping practices has progressed in a very ad-hoc but human focused fashion ever since horse domestication began several thousand years ago. It is not surprising that horsekeeping practices developed in this way; throughout history, horses have been kept as a resource or as a tool, be it for war, agriculture, general transport and as a leisure activity for the wealthy.

Very little thought has been put into how this affects the way we manage the modern domestic horse. For example, the workload for the horse has reduced dramatically; horses are now being confined in increasingly smaller areas as pressure for space grows. They are often fed on feeds that are nutritionally unsuitable for their workload, and increasing awareness in issues such as equine health and welfare, combined with growing concern for 'The Environment' has led to questions being asked about how and why we keep equines the way we do.

Throughout history horses have been kept as a resource or as a tool, be it for war, agriculture or general transport.

It is only in the past few decades that rapid change has come about, not only in the role of the horse, but also in the socio-economic makeup of horse owners. Horses, certainly in the western world, are now used primarily for leisure activities and are owned by people from a huge variety of backgrounds. There are now many new challenges facing contemporary horse owners.

1

The modern domestic horse is much more likely to be kept for leisure purposes than for work. This can have huge implications on the health and well-being of our horses and create heavy demands on our time and resources. We need to rethink how we keep horses today, rather than carry on doing things traditionally simply because that is 'how it has always been done'.

It is clear that something has to change, traditional management systems do not fit into the needs and expectations of modern horsekeeping. We need to ensure that the physiological and behavioural needs of horses are met without compromising the environment and our own lifestyle. This means looking at how and why we keep horses the way we do and acknowledging that there might be a better way; a way that takes care of their needs, takes care of the environment and saves us time, money and energy - all at the same time - a true win-win situation all round.

We need to ensure that their needs are met without compromising the environment and our own lifestyle.

Forward thinking horse owners are beginning to look for alternatives. This book looks at some of the issues facing contemporary horsekeepers *and* the equine community as a whole. It offers solutions, culminating in a total management system designed to address the issues of keeping horses in the 21st century. This is called **The Equicentral System**.

We have been educating horse owners around the world about this *sustainable* system of management for many years now, to great effect. This system integrates natural horse behaviour *and* good land/environmental management and also helps humans through reduced workloads and costs.

Chapter 2: How 'traditional' practices developed

In the last few thousand years of human civilization, horsekeeping has been an integral part of everyday life for many cultures around the world (opinions vary as to exactly how long, but it is thought to be around 5000 years). Indeed, many civilizations were said to have been built from the back of a horse.

Initially, horses were purely an animal to hunt and eat along with other grazing herbivores. At different times in history, many cultures on various continents transitioned to capturing and keeping horses (domesticating them). This was done initially for their meat, skins etc. but then over time, developed to using them as work animals.

Many cultures transitioned to using horses for work instead of or as well as for their meat, skins etc.

Many cultures that first domesticated horses were actually nomadic people, and so the horse became part of this nomadic lifestyle. As these people began to settle and develop agriculture, so too horses began to be more confined, so that humans had more control of them and could access them easily as and when needed. Initially this was done by keeping horses in large 'corrals'.

In cultures that developed farming and remained static, this meant that horses then had to be fed and cared for. At the same time, the manure and urine that these confined horses produced was seen as a valuable fertiliser with which to grow crops. This mirrors the keeping of other farm animals which were also seen as valuable producers of fertiliser, as well as the more obvious producers of meat/wool etc.

As people began to settle and develop agriculture, so too horses began to be more confined.

Horses have been kept in captivity for many centuries now, but the greatest influence on how we keep them in the present day came about in the last few hundred years. Stables, although having existed for many centuries, did not become commonplace until around the 16th century with the advent of urbanisation. As urbanisation developed and huge numbers of people migrated to city living, huge numbers of horses were also moved to the cities.

Stables were a means of keeping horses near to humans so that the horse could be put to work quickly and easily. Indeed, in the rapidly growing cities, areas to turn horses out to pasture were rare.

In those days, horses were the equivalent of the cars, trucks, trains and buses in use today. 'Horse power' was the main form of power before the combustion engine. Therefore in most cases, even though horses were often fully stabled with no access to pasture, they worked many hours a day (often 12 or more). Their stable was a necessary place to rest, recuperate and eat concentrate feed so that they were able and ready to work again the next day.

So, at this time in history, horses existed in various settings; as wild animals (which were still hunted by humans and other predators), as rural work animals (predominantly on farms), as city-living work animals (doing a huge variety of jobs that have now been largely superseded by machinery). A number of horses *were* kept for pleasure, mainly for riding in hunts by the wealthy (aristocracy), but most horses were simply work animals.

The aristocracy were able to employ teams of people (grooms) whose sole responsibility was to ensure that the horses were ready and available for the 'master' or 'mistress' to use at a moment's notice.

Stables were 'space efficient', whether it be in overcrowded cities, on valuable agricultural land or in military camps.

Running parallel with horses being kept as work animals, horses were an integral part of warfare and the military, in fact horses, along with other equines, have always been important for warfare and the world would be a very different place today without them.

The intricate stable management practices that are often still taught today (mainly in Europe) have foundations based on a military system of horsekeeping; they are labour intensive and time consuming. This was not a problem for the army of yesteryear when each recruit usually had just one horse to take care of and the routine and hard work involved was a useful way of instilling discipline and simultaneously taking up the time of these young men.

Military horses were kept both in mobile management systems *and* permanent management systems, with the mobile management systems generally being used when the army was 'in the field' on campaign.

Running parallel with horses being kept as domestic work animals, horses were an integral part of warfare and the military.

Horses were at the forefront of the Agricultural Revolution (mid 1700's). The Agricultural Revolution was the predecessor to the Industrial Revolution (1800's) and was a time of major development in farm machinery (most of it horse drawn). By the end of these periods in history these horse management practices had become entrenched in western culture.

Horses that were used for agriculture were often kept in a more simplistic and efficient manner. A farm horse would be at pasture when pasture was available and would be brought into buildings such as barns and fed hay and grains only when necessary. As their time and resources were usually limited, a farmer had to keep their horses in the most efficient way possible; the horses were part of an integrated management system within the farm. However, as farming techniques progressed and the pressure to glean as much as possible from the land increased, there was usually increased pressure to house working farm horses in as small an area as possible in order to maximise the productive space on the land. This resulted in some working farm horses being stabled for at least part of each year. By-products of cereal production such as straw (for feed and bedding) were used to aid this process.

Stables *also* evolved to provide a relatively warm and sheltered environment for humans to work in while taking care of horses.

Certain styles of stable buildings allow people to handle and care for horses in relative comfort, whilst also protecting them from the elements. 'Barn style' stables are a good example of this, with a central aisle between two enclosed rows of stables and large doors at either end of the building. These large doors can then be opened in warmer weather and closed in colder weather. The horses can usually put their head directly outside for fresh air in better versions of this style of stable building. This style of stable building evolved in parts of the world where the winters are extremely cold (northern Europe e.g. Scandinavia).

Stables also evolved to provide a relatively warm and sheltered environment for humans to work in while taking care of horses.

Over time the 'industry standard' for stable size has become 12ft x 12ft (approximately 3.6m x 3.6m) and this tends to apply whatever the size of the horse. This is a very small area and would not be acceptable for animals that are more often on public display (such as zoo animals). Some horses spend many hours, or even all of their time, in this confined area, so it is not surprising that they can develop abnormal behaviours as a result.

The 'industry standard' for stable size tends to apply whatever the size of the horse.

It is only very recently, and mainly in the Western world, that horses have become predominantly a leisure 'accoutrement' rather than a work animal. This change has become even more pronounced during the last 30 to 40 years and the current situation is that horses now rarely 'work for a living'.

As already mentioned, many of the traditional horsekeeping practices still in use today have developed from practices used hundreds of years ago, long before the first Cruelty to Animals Act of 1876 (in the UK). Traditional management systems were human focused by necessity and did not take the horses' needs into consideration. They were developed in a time before animal welfare was a concept; unsurprising, as this is a relatively new ideology.

Since the legislation was first introduced, many of the animal welfare issues, (including those relating to horses) have been addressed, however there are many more which still need to be examined. As public awareness grows, so we as horse owners need to be proactive in addressing some of these issues.

Animal welfare is a relatively new ideology.

We now have many practices that are both more convenient for humans *and* have been anthropomorphised (which is to ascribe human form or attributes to something), with owners often assuming that their horse's needs are similar to their own.

For example, a horse owner commonly thinks that a 'cosy' stable, warm rugs, meals of high energy feed etc. constitute good horse welfare, because that is what they would want for themselves. They tend to not take the horse's natural behaviour and needs into consideration.

Because humans sometimes find it difficult to see the needs of animals as being different from human needs, they readily fall into the trap of allowing themselves to believe that their horse chooses to live more like a human than a horse.

8

Horse owners commonly think that a cosy stable, warm rugs, meals of high energy feed etc. constitute good horse welfare.

This is why it is so important that horse owners have a good understanding of what natural/normal horse behaviour is and try to apply as much of that knowledge as possible to the way that they manage their horse/s.

Chapter 3: Issues for modern horse owners

There are various issues that face modern horse owners. **These can be loosely grouped into the following four subjects:**

- Horse health and welfare concerns.

- Human factors.

- Horse population issues.

- Land issues.

Horse health and welfare concerns

- Animal welfare is coming under increasing scrutiny in the modern world and what is considered 'good welfare practice' is constantly evolving. Social media continues to increase its influence and some aspects of horse riding and management practices are already coming under close examination on social media outlets.

- Behavioural enrichment is about enhancing the 'lifestyle' of captive animals by providing the environmental stimuli necessary for their optimal psychological and physiological well-being. Concepts such as behavioural enrichment were not even imagined at a time in history when life was generally *very* hard for all but the very wealthy.

- Behavioural enrichment for captive animals has become an absolutely essential practice in modern, well managed zoos, but is still almost unheard of within many areas of horse culture where it is difficult to break through years of traditional practice.

- Add to that the huge variety of different things you can do with a horse, even as a leisure animal, and that each one of those activities has its own ideologies, 'experts' and 'gurus', all readily available at the click of a mouse button and all with their own ideas on how horses should be managed or trained.

- As already mentioned, much of the current 'accepted' way that we keep horses today was developed in a time when animal welfare was not a concept. When the horse was used as a working tool, it was seen simply as that; an asset to physically maintain, but no thought was generally given to the horse's mental state. Issues such as stress, confinement, isolation or pain management were not really considered unless it affected the animal's ability to work. This means that much of the 'culture' of modern horsekeeping that has been assimilated from the past has outdated information and values.

Behavioural enrichment for captive animals has become an absolutely essential practice in modern, well managed zoos, but is still almost unheard of within many areas of horse culture.

Management regimes

- To rug or not to rug, to shoe or go barefoot, to stable or have 24 hour turnout, to allow grazing or to restrict grazing... the list goes on. All have their advocates and at the same time their opponents. How does the modern horse owner decide what to do? Whichever path they choose, they face implications and peer/social media pressure to change to an alternative.

- As pressure on available land increases, there is an increase in the use of stabling. When this is combined with peer pressure and/or the emotional 'rush', many horse owners get from 'tucking their horses up' in a nice 'cosy' stable for the night, you can see how this is happening, but it does have huge implications on the health and well-being of horses, who usually much prefer to be outside (with access to simple shade/shelter) in the company of other horses.

- A further complication is that many horse owners feel that their horse actually 'likes' their stable. One of the reasons that horses can appear to enjoy being stabled is because horses are sometimes keen to get into their stable after they have been turned out for a while. This is because a stable usually contains their concentrate feed so the horse is being positively reinforced each and every time they are led into the stable. Once the feed has been eaten the horse is usually just as keen to leave the stable but by now the door is closed and the horse is fastened in.

- Even when horses are kept or spend some time outdoors, there is an increasing tendency to keep them separated. This is done for a number of reasons; fear that their horse will become injured by another or issues relating to separation anxiety, but also because many horse owners lack the skills/experience to handle or separate individual horses from within a group. Once again this goes against the natural needs of a horse for companionship, but also has huge implications on the management of land.

Much of the 'culture' of modern horsekeeping has been assimilated from the past with outdated information and values.

Information accessibility

- Most horse owners are generally very concerned about the health and welfare of their animals, but do not always know the best place to find good information.
- Many modern day horse owners turn to social media before they consult with professionals about the health and welfare of their horse/s.

Many horse owners get an emotional 'rush' from 'tucking their horses up' in a nice 'cosy' stable for the night.

- Social media provides a wealth of information about horses, however some of that information is incorrect, and much of it is contradictory.
- The more responsible respondents on social media do tend to advise inexperienced horse owners to get professional help if they feel it is necessary, however not all do.

Exercise issues

- Domestic horses are rarely exercised enough on a daily basis; the exception perhaps being some higher level competition horses, although many of these do not get enough of the right kind of exercise, which would be lots of slow, long distance walking rather than very fast, high intensity work. Whilst people might plan to exercise their horse/s daily, everyday life has an unfortunate habit of getting in the way of this ideal.
- Lack of exercise in many domestic horses, combined with feeds that are too high in energy (including certain types of pasture) has led to a sharp rise in conditions such as obesity and its associated conditions (see the section *Common physiological disorders in horses*).
- As domestic horses are kept on increasingly smaller areas of land, natural behaviours that would create movement are being further restricted.

Even when horses are kept or spend some time outdoors, there is an increasing tendency to keep them separated.

- Some people never actually plan to exercise their horse/s because they feel that they get enough exercise when turned out in a paddock but this is often not the case.

- There is an ever increasing number of people who keep horses solely as 'pets', 'companion animals' etc. Even though this does not automatically mean that it will, it does *tend* to lead to health/weight management issues due to them not using enough energy through being used for 'work'.

- Many modern horse owners have several horses and, as the number of horses increases, the time/resources required to attend to the exercise needs of each individual horse decreases.

As domestic horses are kept on increasingly smaller areas of land, natural behaviours that would create movement are being further restricted.

The more horses owned the less time there is available to attend to the exercise needs of each individual horse.

The solutions to most of these issues are covered later in either this book, the other books in the series, or on our website **www.equiculture.com.au**

Human factors

Time management

- In the past, caring for horses was *incorporated* into the working day. People worked with their animals and although most people worked long hours, time spent on animal management was factored in to their working hours.

- Modern horse owners are more likely to have horses *as well* as have a job that is not horse related. Most of their time is spent working away from their horses and this includes time spent getting to and from work. In addition, their horse/s may not even be kept at home. This means that their time to interact with their horse/s is often limited to their own available 'free time'.

- People continue to work relatively long hours, but longer commuting times and increases in alternative leisure opportunities for both themselves and their family eat into their often 'time-poor' lifestyle. Yes people usually have more leisure time today, but there are greater demands on that leisure time, not just for themselves but also for their family. Therefore they have to fit horse care duties in around work, family commitments/activities etc.

Money management

- A recent study showed there is a huge socio-economic range within the horse owning community, but many are at the less wealthy end of this range. In other words, the modern horse owner, who uses horses for leisure, is not generally wealthy. This is in stark contrast to the situation of yesteryear when, if horses were kept for pleasure, it was by the 'gentry' / 'aristocracy'.

- This means that modern horse owners have relatively less to spend than the previous group of people who kept horses solely for recreation. Therefore, unlike their predecessors, modern horse owners do not tend to have 'staff' to do the hard work for them or the money required to help with time/labour intensive practices.

- Times have changed dramatically but it is still a relatively expensive pastime and therefore the average modern horse owner is often short on funds.

- In addition, the emotional attachment that most horse owners have for their horse/s means that they can get into financial strife if and when their financial situation changes. For many horse owners selling their horse is not an option if they run out of funds.

The emotional attachment that most horse owners have for their horse/s means that they can get into financial strife if and when their financial situation changes. For many horse owners selling their horse is not an option if they run out of funds.

Powerful marketing pressure

- Modern horse owners have to deal with powerful marketing that is often aimed at getting them to spend money on things that they do not necessarily need.

- Powerful marketing techniques are such a part of modern life that horse owners do not always realise that they are being 'pushed' into doing things that go against the best interests of their horse/s.

Peer pressure

- Thanks largely to social media, we live in an era that is very public and under constant scrutiny. Everyone has an opinion, but not everyone has knowledge. This causes many horse owners, both those new to horsekeeping and even those with experience, to be heavily influenced by peer pressure. Sometimes this is of benefit, but sometimes it is very harmful.

- In this environment (social media), emotive reactions can often override the voice of reason. Without a good understanding of the requirements of good horsekeeping, combined with conviction and self-confidence, people can be swayed into making poor choices.

- Horses are generally very hardy, efficient animals, but peer pressure on issues such as the use of rugs, stables and feeding regimes can cause an owner to question whether they are 'caring enough' and overcompensate, causing the horse potential harm or stress.

- There are also many 'gurus' in the horse world and their followers tend to copy their favourite riders/trainers and, although these people may be skilled at riding or training, they are not necessarily experts on the management of horses.

- Horse ownership is now generally driven by emotion and passion rather than economics or logic.

Safety concerns

- Horse ownership is on the rise in most parts of the developed and developing world. It is now relatively easy to become involved in horses and this means that there is an increase in horse owners who do not have a background in large animal management.

- This leads to a rise in accident rates due to pure inexperience.

Horses are generally very hardy, efficient animals, but peer pressure on issues such as the use of rugs, stables and feeding regimes can cause an owner to question whether they are 'caring enough'.

The solutions to most of these issues are covered later in either this book, the other books in the series, or on our website **www.equiculture.com.au**. In particular see the **Equiculture website Horses and safety page** for links to much more information about safety **www.equiculture.com.au/horses-and safety.html**

Horse over population issues

High number of horses

- There are huge numbers of domestic and naturally-living equines in the world; about 43 million donkeys and 58 million horses worldwide according to Food and Agriculture Organization of the United Nations statistics.

- Most of the developed countries now have *huge* numbers of 'unwanted' horses.

- A higher human population tends to produce (breed) more horses.

- When downturns occur in the economy, many horses are abandoned, and this puts more pressure on the already over stretched equine welfare groups.

A higher human population tends to produce (breed) more horses.

- Modern domestic horses have a long life span, often living for thirty years or more, therefore even if the breeder plans to keep that horse 'for ever', they cannot predict what their life (e.g. their economic status), and therefore the life of that horse, will be like so far into the future.

- In most western countries, disposing of unwanted/unneeded horses by means such having them 'processed' for meat or even 'putting them to sleep' is not seen as an option for anything other than horses at the very end of their life.

- Many horses are 'retired' at about 20 years of age, meaning that they have to be kept, in retirement, for many years.

- It is not only the number of horses that is an issue, but there is usually a variety of types and sizes within a domestic herd. For example, a typical family that has horses may have a children's pony (perhaps a Shetland), an adult riding horse and perhaps a retired schoolmaster. All these horses have very different nutritional and management needs, which may result in some unhealthy compromises in the management of some of them.

It is not only the number of horses that is an issue, but there is usually a variety of types and sizes within a domestic herd.

Overstocking

- Horse owners sometimes end up with several horses to take care of even though they may only be 'using' one of them. This is because horses are often retired due to soundness issues that prevent them from performing at the level required by their owner, yet they still live for many years after this time. So, it is not uncommon for someone to have one riding horse *and* various other horses.

- People with their own land feel the pressure to take on more horses, particularly because there are now so many unwanted horses around. Peer pressure adds to this; there is now a growing culture of 'rescuing' horses. Some people end up over faced and overwhelmed with what they have taken on, but due to 'peer pressure' find it difficult to backtrack.

- Horses are now relatively cheaper to buy than at any other time in history. This means that people are more likely to end up with too many horses to take care of.

- Livery yards (boarding/agistment facilities) frequently overstock their properties in an attempt to maximise the income on the land.

- Overstocking leads to land degradation issues and less feed availability. It is very easy to become 'over-stocked' with horses; therefore it is imperative that horse owners manage the land as well as possible so that it can continue to feed their horses.

Overstocking leads to land degradation issues and less feed availability.

Over breeding

- Some horse owners want to breed for no other reason than they would like their horse to have a foal and they themselves would like to experience all of the emotive triggers associated with caring for a young animal.

- Other horse owners own studs as an economic venture to justify their personal breeding program. While for some this is viable, for many it is not.

- In some countries there are tax incentives associated with breeding horses, leading to some people breeding for the wrong reasons.

- Breeders do not often consider the practicalities of breeding horses that have not evolved to be kept in certain environments. For example, horses that originally evolved in northern, very harsh environments being bred to be kept in warmer climates with mild winters (and usually on lush pasture). These horses in particular need knowledgeable owners that can manage these animals in often inappropriate conditions.

Some horse owners want to breed for no other reason than they would like their horse to have a foal.

- In the past, horses were usually bred for their ability to do a job, but now many are bred for their looks, colour, breed or size (e.g. miniature horses). When animals are bred for certain 'desirable' traits, a surplus of horses are created because some do not 'make the grade', adding to the already large numbers of unwanted horses.

- There is a further issue in regard to breeding relating to the management of stallions. Traditionally, stallions are kept alone and this leads to huge welfare implications. Some stallion owners are moving away from this style of management however many are not. Many horse owners do not have the knowledge and experience required to keep a stallion.

Human hoarding behaviour

- There is a human behavioural condition termed 'animal hoarding'. One definition of animal hoarding is 'a pathological human behaviour that involves a compulsive need to obtain and control animals, coupled with a failure to recognize their suffering'.

- Some hoarders are former breeders who have ceased selling and caring for their animals, while others will claim to be breeders as a psychological defence mechanism, or in hopes of forestalling intervention.
- Some horse owners become fixated on breeding certain types of horses and their argument is that they are breeding something particularly 'unique' when often they are not.

High turnover of horses

- While many horse owners keep horses for many years, even when they are no longer using them, others turnover horses at a high rate.
- Small ponies, such as Shetlands and the smaller breeds of Welsh Ponies, have a particularly high turnover rate because children rapidly grow out of them.
- These ponies are particularly likely to belong to people with little experience due to their small size making them sought out by new horse owners for young children.
- These small breeds are particularly difficult to manage in terms of weight management, and unfortunately, just as their relatively new owners start to become more experienced, the pony is passed on to another, usually inexperienced family, because the current child has grown out of them.

Small ponies have a particularly high turnover rate because children rapidly grow out of them.

- Alternatively, some owners do not pass them on (rehome or sell) but simply do nothing with them.
- As a consequence of these factors these small ponies have an even higher rate of weight management issues than other horse types.
- Many horses are at risk of being passed on frequently. Some horse owners, on encountering problems with a particular horse, simply move on to the next

horse, without first investigating whether their own skills could be improved by further education.

- This high turnover also has an effect on the stability of a herd; individual horses lose their companions and new horses have to establish themselves within a new group, sometimes resulting in conflict.

—

The solutions to most of these issues are covered later in either this book, the other books in the series, or on our website **www.equiculture.com.au**

—

Land issues

Environmental issues

- Taking care of 'The Environment' is a relatively modern notion. Even though this was not a concept in itself many years ago, in the pre-industrialised age horse-keeping was more 'environmentally friendly' than today, in much the same way that farming was. Farmers *had* to know how to keep their land healthy and productive in order to sustain their livestock and their families. Furthermore, they had to do this without the help of chemical fertilisers, herbicides and pesticides.

- Taking care of the environment is increasingly gaining importance. Horse owners have been slow to include this factor into their management systems, partly due to the lack of information that is available about how to keep horses in a way that is not detrimental to the environment.

- Many horse owners *are* concerned about environmental issues and just need to be given information about how they can keep horses in a way that actually enhances the wider environment.

Lack of land availability

- Most horse owners aspire to owning their own land, but for many this is just not possible.

- Land for grazing is becoming increasingly more expensive as the human population grows.

- More people means that more food has to be produced. In turn more houses and their related infrastructure have to be built. This all uses up more land and makes what is left relatively more valuable and expensive.

- Horse owners are often desperate for somewhere to keep their horses. The increased need for land for horses often results in unsuitable land being leased/sold to horse owners. The area maybe too small, the land may be too wet/dry, too steep, flood prone etc. but this does not stop real estate agents or landlords from enticing horse owners to the property; after all horse owners are a lucrative market.

Most horse owners are concerned about environmental issues and just need to be given information about how they can keep horses in a way that actually enhances the wider environment.

- Many horse owners actually migrate to other countries in order to have land for horsekeeping and some move to other areas within their own country. This may or may not be a problem in itself, but it can cause family pressures unless all of the family members are in agreement with the move.

Lack of land management skills

- Many horse owners do not have a land management background. Horse owners often start life in the city or suburbia, and then move to acreage simply *because* of their interest in horses.

- Even those horse owners *with* a rural background may base their horse and pasture management systems on certain traditional and modern farming practices, such as aiming for high energy grasses which are developed for rapid weight gain or milk production in cattle.

- It is even quite common for experienced and professional horse people to have no real understanding of land care. Horse owners tend to be highly focused on their horses, but the pasture side of horse management is often put in the 'too hard' basket. Degraded pasture is frequently believed to be an unfortunate, but inevitable, consequence of domestic horsekeeping.
- This adds to the reputation of horse owners being poor land managers.

The increased need for land for horses often results in unsuitable land being leased/sold to horse owners. The area maybe too small, the land may be too wet/dry, too steep, flood prone etc.

Incorrect mind-set/beliefs

- Paddocks are often regarded simply as somewhere for horses to exercise rather than as a valuable resource. Land for horses is often badly managed and under, or over, used.

- There is also a common belief that pasture is not good or is even dangerous for certain types of horses. Owners of horses that tend to get fat and/or have metabolic disorders sometimes struggle with the often conflicting information that is available to them.

- Much of the information that is readily available about pasture and horses is outdated.

- This information comes from a time when horses worked for a living and before certain pasture plants e.g. ryegrass, had been selectively bred to be very high in energy.

- This means that many horses are being kept on land that contains dangerous plant species and these horses are at risk of obesity and its related conditions.

Much of the information that is readily available about pasture and horses is outdated.

Public perception concerns

- Horsekeeping is increasingly coming under public scrutiny; what a horse owner does with their horses and their land in terms of noise, pollution, aesthetics etc. is attracting the attention of local authorities and environmental agencies, with increasing pressure for legislation.

- Some local authorities (in various parts of the world) are discussing legislative options, even though other local authorities positively welcome horse owners with open arms, as they see them as an economic asset to an area.

- The public are quite rightly concerned if land in their area is a haven for weeds and mud, and appears to be fenced entirely by knotted, loose, white electric tape. Because of this, horse owners are sometimes seen as 'land vandals' by other members of the community, due to poor land management skills. Not only does this degrade the land e.g. bare soil, weeds etc. and give horse owners a bad reputation, it also leads to many other issues that affect the wider environment. Horse owners need to be aware, for example, that poor land management affects water quality. Soil and manure washes off a badly

27

managed horse property and this can severely affect water quality in local streams, rivers, estuaries and eventually the sea.

- It is not only the lifestyle of residential neighbours that can be affected by a badly managed horse property, such a property can also have an effect on a local businesses. Poor aesthetics, dust, flies etc. may put customers off.

- Horses are seen by other animal managers (farmers) as being 'fussy' grazers and as being detrimental to having good pasture. Even though there is some truth in these beliefs, the detrimental effects that horses have on pasture can all be overcome with good management. In fact in some countries, equines are being used for grassland conservation work because their grazing style and behaviour is beneficial for recreating or maintaining biodiverse grasslands. Even in countries such as Australia, where equines are not indigenous, the types of plants that equines thrive on are the types of plants that are now gaining interest in both conservation and agricultural situations - native grasses.

Horse owners are sometimes seen as 'land vandals' by other members of the community, due to poor land management skills.

Manure management issues

- Manure is now seen as a nuisance in some parts of the world where horses are kept. This means that some local authorities are increasing legislation about how it must be handled and disposed of. A horse owner needs to familiarise themselves with their local laws regarding the handling, storage and disposal of horse manure because regulations vary widely as to what can and cannot be done with it. Generally, the closer the land is to an urban area, the more regulations there will be. This also varies hugely from country to country.

● Horse owners themselves are confused about what to do with manure with regards to parasitic worm management issues.

—

See the second book in this series *The Equicentral System Series Book 2 - Healthy Land, Healthy Pasture, Healthy Horses* for in-depth information about manure management.

—

The way forward

H orse O wners need to be R esponsible, S ustainable and E thical

The main considerations:

- We need to understand about what horses *really* are and what constitutes good management of them; in particular with regards their *mental health*. As we become more aware of both the physical *and* mental needs of horse/s, we may have to make changes in our management practices to ensure both are being met.

- Domestic horses need to be provided with an environment that is as close to natural as possible so that they can carry out most of their normal behaviours. This is not difficult to do and does not necessarily mean that we have to forego doing the things that we enjoy about owning horses.

Domestic horses need to be provided with an environment that is as close to natural as possible so that they can carry out most of their normal behaviours.

- Horse/s must receive sufficient exercise; horses have evolved to have a lifestyle that requires movement, and lots of it. We need to find ways to use up their energy and get them to burn up their excess fat. We have to acknowledge that under-exercising can be just as harmful as overwork, but in a different way. See the section *Ideas for extra exercise*.

- Most horse owners have a limited amount of time. We need to manage our precious time and avoid wasting energy on doing the wrong things. By doing this, we can make sure that any time that we do spend with our horse/s can be 'quality time'.

- Most horse owners have a limited amount of money to spend. This makes it imperative that we do not waste money on things that we do not need to buy and that we maximise 'value for money' on the things we do need to buy.

- We need to be certain that we are not doing things simply because 'that is the way it has always been done', or because we are being bamboozled into it by strong marketing practices. We need to keep an open mind at all times and try not to be swayed if we feel that the advice we are receiving is wrong.

- We need to think very carefully before breeding and adding to the already large population of horses. We also need to make sure that we can afford the time money and space that additional horses will require if we are planning to increase our herd.

- Whilst it is possible to keep horses in various climates and conditions, we need to accept that our chosen breed/type may struggle to cope in an unsuitable environment and we will have to adjust our management system to suit.

- We need to be practical about our choice of horse, matching the right breed/type for the 'job' we have in mind. We also have to be realistic about our level of experience.

- We need to be responsible, proactive custodians of the land and become good role models of land stewardship. Horse properties can be an economic and environmental asset to a community if managed well.

Horse properties can be an economic and environmental asset to a community if managed well.

- We need to manage horses and the land that they occupy in a way that is as 'environmentally friendly' and therefore land friendly as possible. The good news is; it is quite possible and very beneficial for all concerned, to manage the land that horses are kept on as part of a healthy ecosystem.

- Rather than looking to procure more land, we usually need to maximise production on the land we already have, because buying/leasing more may not be possible. This does not mean overstocking the land, it means improving the management (and production capacity) of the land that we have available. In many cases, horse owners can vastly improve on what they are currently doing; they just need to learn how.

- We need to make sure that we are managing our horse manure in a way that is sustainable *and* fits in with local regulations. Most horse owners can improve how they manage their horse manure.

—

See the second book in this series *The Equicentral System Series Book 2 - Healthy Land, Healthy Pasture, Healthy Horses* for in-depth information about manure management.

—

- We need to design horse facilities that are safer and more 'user friendly' for both horse handlers and horses. Safe practices are very important not only for ethical reasons, but also for duty of care and litigation reasons.

—

See the third book in this series *The Equicentral System Series Book 3 – Horse Property Planning and Development* for more information about safe horse facilities.

—

- We need to respond proactively rather than reactively to the changes that have occurred to horsekeeping and bring it into the 21st century. This sometimes involves 'thinking outside the box' in terms of looking at innovative ways of keeping horses.

Above all we need to adopt sustainable horsekeeping systems.

We need to design horse facilities that are safer and more 'user friendly' for both horse handlers and horses.

Source - Sally Mitchell at Sally Mitchell Equestrian - UK.

Sustainable horsekeeping

The dictionary definition of sustainability is 'able to be maintained at a certain rate or level'. However, sustainability can be a very divisive word in many circles. It is an important concept that affects everybody, but what does it mean in the horse world?

Of course, sustainability is about the environment, reducing soil loss, maintaining clean water, providing habitat for flora and fauna etc., but, to us it is *also* about examining the *lifestyle* of both the horse owner and their horse/s and seeing if any improvements can be made. It is important to understand how, by making small but significant changes, we can reap huge benefits to our own equine lifestyle and at the same time we can have a positive affect the wider environment.

Sustainability (or sustainable horsekeeping) means different things to different people. At Equiculture, we see sustainable horsekeeping as being a means to maintain your equine lifestyle efficiently using a combination of various factors **such as:**

- **Horse health and welfare considerations** – not only for ethical reasons, but a stressed, unhealthy horse is likely to be dangerous and it will eventually break down either mentally, physically or both.

- **Ease of use** - if it is too difficult you cannot keep doing it; if your management practices are very time consuming, you will have very little time to enjoy your relationship with your horse/s.

34

- **Sound economics** - if you cannot afford to keep doing it something will eventually have to give; if your horsekeeping practices require that you have to work extra hours or a second job just to be able to afford to keep horses, then this cannot usually be sustained in the long term.

- **Relationship balance** - if your horsekeeping practices are adversely affecting your other personal relationships, something will eventually begin to suffer.

- **Environmental considerations** – if you do not take care of the environment then the environment cannot take care of you and yours. By adding to land degradation, soil loss, pollution of the waterways etc. then eventually there will be nothing left worth having. We have to be responsible land stewards.

- **Community perception** – if you are creating a poor impression of horsekeeping then, in time, horsekeeping will be restricted by legislation.

—

Soil loss and pollution from nutrients is a huge problem in the modern world. For example, the UK has lost **80%** of its top soil since 1850! Nutrients from animal manure and fertilisers cause devastation to marine life. As well as reducing or eliminating soil loss, good horse and land management results in an *increase* of soil depth on a horse property (by retaining nutrients which in turn increase the amount of organic matter through better plant growth).

—

By adding to land degradation, soil loss, pollution of the waterways etc. then eventually there will be nothing left worth having. We have to be responsible land stewards.

Why is sustainability so important?

- The only way you can design for permanence, long term stability and resilience against fluctuations in resources, changes within your life, outside influences, etc., is to mimic nature as closely as possible in terms of diversity, and functionality; something that is fairly simple in many senses. However, we have to accept that, in almost all cases, you cannot keep a domestic horse 100% naturally and therefore compromises have to be made. The skill lies in knowing which compromises can be made.

- As previously mentioned, in many areas around the world, some local/state or federal authorities are justifiably looking at ways of dealing with irresponsible land management practices adopted by many horse property owners. The current situation is not sustainable and horse owners need to be responsible and take ownership of the environmental issues caused by horsekeeping before the inevitable legislation occurs. Horse ownership should be thought of as a privilege, not a right.

The benefits of utilising sustainable thinking

- By making the whole of your equine practices more sustainable, you reduce your costs and workload and increase available feed on your land, resulting in you being able to spend quality time with your family and your horses. The land not only becomes more productive, but also has improved aesthetics.

By making the whole of your equine practices more sustainable, you reduce your costs and workload and increase available feed on your land.

- Looking at an area of land as a self-sustaining ecosystem has many health benefits for your horse/s. The horse's lifestyle will be as close to natural as possible in a domestic situation. Complimentary systems within the pasture work together to provide a healthy biodiverse environment for your horse/s to live in. These natural systems provide a wide range of healthy plants for your horse/s to graze upon, once again mimicking the horse's natural environment.

- By doing so, horse owners ensure not only the health of the environment, but also the on-going viability of their love of keeping horses. We understand that there are areas of potential conflict between some environmentalists and some horse owners, but there need not be. The interests of these groups are not mutually exclusive and can in fact be very compatible indeed. Horse owners need to take responsibility and adopt sustainable practices for their own benefit, the benefit of future horse keepers, the benefit of their horses, their property and the environment as a whole.

Problems/barriers to sustainable horsekeeping

- Naturally-living equines have access to very large tracts of land, many square kilometres/miles, and their normal behaviour reflects this. When we keep horses in captivity, they are generally restricted to paddocks that are small (by horse standards). So we have to pro-actively manage domestic horses, in particular some of their behavioural 'quirks', otherwise they will quickly degrade the land.

- By keeping horses 'domestically', we change some of their behaviours, along with their diets and their social interactions. Part of being a responsible sustainable and ethical horse owner is to ensure that these changes have no or minimal impact on the health and well-being of the horses you have chosen to become responsible for. After all you chose them; they did not volunteer to become your responsibility.

Looking at an area of land as a self-sustaining ecosystem has many health benefits for your horse/s.

How can we achieve sustainability?

- The simplest way to create a healthy sustainable lifestyle for your horse/s is to try to work with nature and mimic natural systems as best you can by using informed compromises, rather than trying to work against it.

- People talk about 'natural' horsekeeping systems; unfortunately, unless you are fortunate enough to have several hundred acres/hectares to let your horses roam on, this is unachievable and some compromises have to be made. If we attempt to compromise the environment, imbalances occur. The environment relies on complex ecosystems and, when gaps occur in these ecosystems, problems develop.

- Sustainable horsekeeping is about making a lifestyle choice - it is a system that encourages the horse owner to work with natural processes to create healthy pasture for a healthy horse that also conserves resources such as soil and water, whilst minimising environmental impact. The system becomes resilient and self-regulating, and the equine lifestyle is maintained.

The simplest way to create a healthy sustainable lifestyle for your horse/s is to try to work with nature and mimic natural systems as best you can by using informed compromises.

See your horse as part of an ecosystem

To summarise, the Equiculture approach is that you should see your horse/s *as part of an ecosystem*, not *separate to it*. If you see the horse in a more holistic way, as part of the ecosystem in which it lives, then your horse/s will benefit from living in a healthier environment. In order to do this, you need to understand what issues you are facing and how you can address them.

Every horse owner should be looking to improve their land management skills, whether they own *or* lease the land that their horse/s live on or not. Improving land management skills has numerous benefits **such as:**

- The land will produce more feed for your horses – this will save you time and money.

- The land will become more valuable – important if you own the land.

- The owner of the land (if it is not you) will be more likely to carry on leasing that land to you.

- The land will become more 'environmentally friendly' and you and your horse/s will reap the benefits.

The land will produce more feed for your horses – this will save you time and money.

Chapter 4: Horse behaviour, welfare and lifestyle

In this age of enlightenment, more and more people are willing to improve the lifestyle of their horse, both for the associated welfare benefits *and* the improvements in performance that result from a healthier, and arguably happier, horse. There is, however, confusion about what horses really need.

In order to learn how a domestic horse should behave, we actually need to start with learning about the behaviour of naturally-living horses. We cannot surmise what normal horse behaviour is by watching domestic horses, because these horses have to modify their behaviour due to man-made constraints such as fences, feed times and so on. In a natural setting, horses carry out behaviours without being hampered by such constraints.

At the same time, whilst it is an idyllic notion that we can keep our horses as 'naturally' as possible, the reality is that, unless you own hundreds, if not thousands of acres/hectares of land, this is not possible. However, we do owe it to domestic horses to acknowledge their behaviour and understand how they fit into their natural environment as best we can. We can then use this knowledge to create as natural an environment *as possible* in the domestic situation, whilst at the same time accepting that we will have to make certain compromises on our 2/5/10/100 acre/hectare area of land. These compromises are necessary to enable our horses to thrive in an artificial environment.

There is a lot of information available about how horse behaviour relates to training, but not as much information is available about how horse behaviour relates to their management. In fact, as already mentioned, the horse world is not even as forward thinking as many modern zoos in numerous respects and 'tradition' plays a part in holding back change. Much of the available information about horse management is based on outdated beliefs and practices that came about long before the behaviour and physiology of horses were researched scientifically or even considered important. Despite relatively recent research findings that disprove much of this outdated information about horses, old beliefs are, unfortunately, still entrenched in the 'culture' of the horse world.

From various scientific studies we know how equines behave when living wild or feral (escaped/released into a naturally-living situation). We also know that domestic horses retain their 'wild' characteristics because, in cases where they have been released or have escaped (for example Mustangs in the USA and Brumbies in Australia), they have survived and thrived. This tells us that they still possess their natural behaviours. We also know that when animals are prevented from carrying out their natural behaviours, they can become stressed, and that this affects their behaviour and health. All animals, including zoo animals, domestic animals and indeed humans, develop behavioural and physiological problems if their lifestyle is inadequate and prevents them from carrying out basic yet fundamental behaviours.

Much of the available information about horse management is based on outdated beliefs and practices that came about long before the behaviour and physiology of horses were researched scientifically or even considered important.

Nature has usually managed to find a good solution to most problems. We need to study natural systems to see what we can learn and perhaps implement from them.

We need to study natural systems to see what we can learn and perhaps implement from them.

Naturally-living v domestic-living horses

Naturally-living (wild/feral) horses have a very different lifestyle to domestic horses. This section compares the lifestyle of naturally-living v domestic-living horses so that you can better understand why horses can struggle to cope in the domestic situation. When you understand what is really important to a horse, it is possible to change the way you keep them so that many of their needs are met.

Herd/band life differences:

- **Naturally-living horses** are highly social animals and therefore they live in herds/bands meaning they have rich and varied social lives which include activities such as sexual behaviour, play behaviour and mutual grooming behaviour. Actual fights are rare in established groups, with threats or gestures being more common.

Naturally-living horses are highly social animals and therefore they live in herds/bands.

- **Domestic-living horses** are often prevented from interacting with other horses which can cause high levels of stress in an animal that would never be alone by choice. Many horses, in addition to being stabled in a way that prevents them from touching and sometime even seeing another horse, are also turned out separately from other horses. In short, some horses are *never* allowed to interact with another horse; they are unable carry out behaviours which allows them to form the social bonds that are so important to them. As a result of this, they cannot learn behavioural rules from peers, friends and relatives, and so struggle to interact successfully if and when they *are* introduced to other horses. Although we should not anthropomorphise, sometimes it is difficult for people to fully understand the implications of their actions without doing so. Imagine what it must be like to *never* interact socially with fellow humans? Imagine what this must be like for an animal that evolved to live as part of a herd?

Many horses, in addition to being stabled in a way that prevents them from touching and sometime even seeing another horse, are also turned out separately from other horses.

Group decisions and choice differences:

- **Naturally-living horses** are able to make group *and* individual decisions about where they want to be throughout the day. When the weather is hot or inclement, they can choose to seek out shade/shelter, they can choose when to begin grazing and when to snooze, they can choose when to go to higher ground or lower ground and they can choose their own companions from within the herd that they live in or they can choose how much individual space they need.

- **Domestic-living horses** usually have no control over where they are at any point in their lives; they may be confined in a stable 24/7 or have 'free' access to grassy pasture, but their range is always restricted by walls or fences. They may be unable to get to higher/drier ground if necessary so may be forced to stand for hours in muddy conditions when the weather is wet. Likewise, if they are turned out in an area without shade/shelter, they are unable to do anything about the situation if the weather is very hot or inclement. They are *totally* reliant on humans for water, food, shade and shelter and they cannot usually choose their own companions.

Domestic-living horses usually have no control over where they are at any point in their lives, their range is always restricted by walls or fences.

Companionship differences:

- **Naturally-living horses** may 'pair bond' with another horse in the group that is similar in age, size and sex. These bonds are often for life. Most naturally-living horse herds, once established, are much more consistent than domestic groups. They tend to stay together for many years or indeed, for life.

- **Domestic-living horses** are frequently keep alone. Those that are not may form bonds with other horses but these relationships can be changed/severed at any time. Settled herds of domestic horses tend to be more passive if the group members are reasonably constant. A group which has constantly changing members (because horses are being removed or added to the herd) will tend to be less secure.

Stereotypic behaviour differences:

- **Naturally-living horses** do not develop the stereotypic behaviours that are common in domestic horses (stereotypic behaviours are defined as repetitive, invariant behaviour patterns with no obvious goal or function).

Domestic-living horses are usually unable to select their own companions and any relationships they do make with other horses can be changed/severed at any time.

- **Domestic-living horses** can show many stereotypic behaviours if managed inappropriately and these are unfortunately termed 'vices' in the horse world. These behaviours usually come about as a response to inappropriate living conditions.

Domestic-living horses can show many stereotypic behaviours if managed inappropriately.

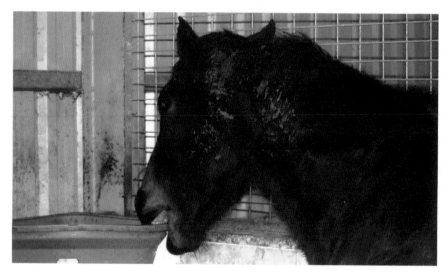

Reproduction differences:

- **Naturally-living horses** reproduce regularly. Mares produce a foal most years, and this means that mares are usually pregnant with another foal while feeding a current foal at foot. Milk production requires huge amounts of energy which she can only get from eating as much as possible and by using up stored body fat if necessary. Stallions work hard to keep their mares together and stay extra alert for any would be rivals for their position. Energy is also required to serve (mate) their mares when they are 'in season'. Some stallions even share a herd whilst others never have a herd of their own and remain part of a bachelor group. Stallions have an important role in the upbringing of foals and their demeanour has an effect on the health of the foal. Generally, the calmer the stallion, the more settled the herd and stronger and healthier the offspring. This is mainly due to the foals being able to rest and eat without constantly being disturbed by conflict.

Naturally-living mares produce a foal most years, or two out of every three years, and this means that mares are usually pregnant with another foal while feeding a current foal at foot.

- **Domestic-living horses** do not usually use energy for reproduction. This is just as well because there are already huge numbers of domestic and naturallyliving equines in the world. However, we need to remember that domestic horses do not have this natural drain on their energy and feed them accordingly. Usually, domestic stallions are kept totally separate from other horses, creating anxiety for them and land management issues for the owner (tracking lines near fences etc.). Domestic stallions are also rarely involved in the raising of their foals.

Weaning differences:

- **Naturally-living horses** wean their young over a relatively long period and it does not usually occur until the youngster is at least one year old (when the mare has another foal) but can actually be later. If the mare does not have a foal in the year following, she may allow the youngster to carry on suckling into their second year. She may allow this to happen even if she does have another foal (and is pregnant with the next); there are no hard and fast rules and many variations are seen. Youngsters are weaned gradually over an extended period.

- **Domestic-living horses** usually go through an unnatural weaning process which involves being separated from other horses when very young (around five to six months) which is stressful in itself. Weaning methods vary, but they usually involve a foal being suddenly and totally separated from their dam. This means that the foal has to cope without the comforting presence of their dam *and* without being able to suckle, all at the same time. Unnatural weaning is thought to lead to behavioural issues, such as separation anxiety, later in life.

Alert behaviour differences:

- **Naturally-living horses** are on the alert for many hours a day, although this behaviour is shared with other members of the herd. This is one of the most important reasons that grazing animals live in herds, otherwise they would have to be permanently vigilant and would eventually become exhausted. Even when not particularly alert, they are able to become alert very quickly and react with lightning speed to danger if necessary. Horses take it in turn to be 'on guard' whilst others in the herd eat or sleep.

- **Domestic-living horses** are not usually in danger from predators etc. but they do not know this. They feel safer in a herd because they can then share 'looking out for danger' between herd members. If they are kept alone, this can result in them living in a permanently stressed state. Many domestic horses, especially those kept alone, develop what is termed 'learned helplessness'. This is their body and minds way of 'shutting down' in order to prevent stress overload. The horse cannot continue to be in a state of constant stress so it reluctantly accepts its current status. The owner assumes that the horse is happy to be alone as it makes no easily observable signals that it is stressed, when in reality the horse has no choice but to accept its situation. If and when an owner tries to address this by putting the horse with a companion, the initial response from the horse is often to display loud, very excitable behaviour which can appear hostile and aggressive. This may be the case for some horses that have been unable to learn correct social skills or have become mentally damaged by inappropriate management in the past. In most cases, these behaviours soon calm down and the result is a much more mentally positive environment for the horse.

An initial response can be excitable behaviour which can appear hostile and aggressive.

Diet/nutrition differences:

- **Naturally-living horses** eat a very high fibre/low sugar/low starch/low protein diet and graze or forage for many hours a day.

- **Domestic-living horses** usually eat the same nutrients throughout the year and often have a diet that is inappropriately high in energy and too low in fibrous roughage. This results in a much shorter period of the day being spent eating/chewing. In fact, many domestic horses spend less than five hours per day chewing. The pasture that domestic horses have access to often contains many weeds and/or unsuitable grasses. Sometimes this pasture is classed as 'improved' pasture, but it only contains plants that are too high in energy for most horses. The term 'improved' when applied to grasses and pasture means plants that have been developed (bred) for the much higher energy needs of beef and dairy cattle. Domestic horses often have a much less diverse mixture of plants to graze/browse on, but conversely horse owners frequently 'micro manage' their horse's daily intake with a wide variety of very carefully measured out supplements.

Weight gain and weight loss cycle differences:

- **Naturally-living horses** go through cycles of gaining and losing weight throughout the various seasons of the year. This causes them to 'overeat' during the good times to put down a layer of fat which enables them to survive the leaner times. In winter or drought, they lose the excess weight that they gained in the good times; this regulates their behaviour and internal biochemistry and enables them to survive the variations in the availability of nutrients.

- **Domestic-living horses** still have the same genetic makeup as their naturally living relatives, with the same innate need to eat more when food is readily available, but they are usually 'micro managed' so that they maintain the same weight throughout the year, rather than losing a little over winter. This can be a problem because it means that they are already in 'good' condition when pasture is starting to re-grow in the spring/wet season and their internal biochemistry has not been 'reset'. Therefore domestic horses are much more susceptible to obesity related disorders.

Horse owners frequently 'micro-manage' their horse's daily intake with a wide variety of very carefully measured out supplements.

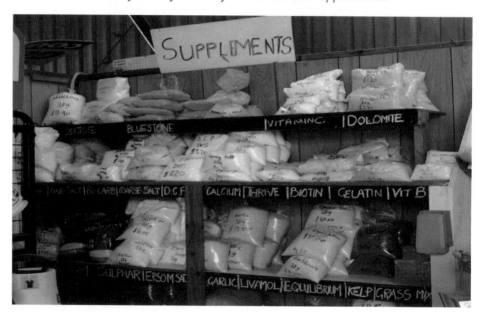

Movement differences:

- **Naturally-living horses** travel large distances on a daily basis, from feed to water and back again in what is known as the 'home-range' (a large area that contains the resources that they need e.g. food/water/shade/shelter). This means that they stay in the same area rather than moving huge distances as some migratory grazing animals do. This does not, however, mean that they do not move much; naturally-living horses often travel around 20 miles (32km) a day and can travel a lot further if necessary, it all depends on various factors. Horses walk continuously whilst grazing and also have to travel between their water source and the areas where food can be found. This is due to the fact that the plants nearest the water hole are always the first to be eaten and horses, therefore, have to travel much further in winter months or times of drought than they do in times of plenty. If food and water is scarce, their home-range will tend to be larger and, conversely, if food and water is abundant, their home-range tends to be smaller, but still much larger than the average horse property. Naturally-living horses do not travel large distances for the sake of it, they travel simply to find enough of the right kinds of food (and enough water). It is thought that fibre collection is the biggest motivation for this movement, rather than nutritional value.

Domestic-living horses are usually already in 'good' condition when pasture is starting to re-grow in the spring.

- **Domestic-living horses** often receive too little exercise and, instead of having to find their own food and water, it is given to them 'on a plate'. A domestic horse does not usually have to travel very far (sometimes not at all in the case of a fully stabled/yarded horse) during each day and night to eat and drink. This is all dependent on the type of pasture they are kept on. In the domestic situation, a horse will walk continuously while grazing if they are turned out on good biodiverse pasture, but, if they are turned out on poor or bare pasture, they do not move much at all, because grazing and walking are linked behaviours - without plants to graze, a horse sees little point in moving and they will miss out on the benefits of lots of slow, steady movement.

A domestic-living horse does not usually have to travel very far (sometimes not at all in the case of a fully stabled/yarded horse) during each day and night to eat and drink.

Hoof wear differences:

- **Naturally-living horses** wear down their hooves by moving across a variety of terrains ranging from soft and wet to abrasive and dry. In addition to wearing their hooves, all this movement also benefits their circulation whilst the constant contraction and expansion of the hooves as they leave the ground and touch down again helps to push blood and lymphatic fluid back up the legs to the body.

- **Domestic-living horses** rarely get enough movement over a varied terrain to keep their hooves in good condition and therefore have to rely on humans to keep their feet in good order. Many domestic horses do not, however, receive adequate hoof care to ensure their feet remain in a good condition. Stabled horses do not benefit from the effects of movement and can suffer with 'filled' or swollen legs caused by retention of blood and lymph fluid.

Temperature/weather differences:

- **Naturally-living horses** cope with a variety of climates and changing seasons ranging from very cold and wet, to very hot and dry and everything in between. They utilise their stores of body fat in hard times and utilise their thicker winter coat to protect themselves in extreme weather conditions. In hot weather, horses use a lot of energy to cool themselves because their large body and, although they are slow to heat up, it takes them a long time to cool down. Horses, like humans, use sweat to cool the body. They also move to and from shelter in adverse weather conditions, which may not always be where the food is, thus increasing movement. In extreme conditions, some types of horse can even go into a state of semi-hibernation in order to preserve energy.

Many domestic-living horses do not receive adequate hoof care to ensure their feet remain in a good condition.

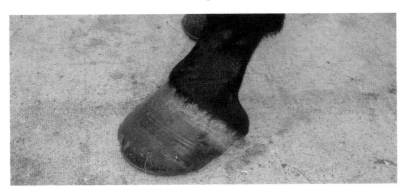

- **Domestic-living horses** rarely have to deal with temperature extremes. Modern rugs and stables result in many domestic horses never experiencing the need to use energy to keep warm. Domestic horses are often inappropriately rugged and/or stabled even when the weather is warm; causing them stress. There *are* some factors that warrant the use of rugs, especially in older horses during inclement weather when they can no longer maintain enough body fat to keep themselves warm, but whenever possible rugs should not take the place of shade/shelter.

Rugs should not take the place of shade/shelter.

Life span differences:

- **Naturally-living horses** tend to have a shorter life span than domestic horses. There are several reasons for this. Even though predators are not usually a factor because their predators have largely been hunted out from the areas in which they live, the environments that they live in are harsher and their teeth tend to wear out sooner. They cannot survive past the stage when their teeth have worn out as they are then no longer able to graze. In most cases, naturally-living horses have a life span of around eight to ten years although the figure varies greatly from situation to situation.

- **Domestic-living horses** generally live much longer. In fact, it is not uncommon for them to reach their thirties and forties. Domestic horses are able to have dental care and are able to be kept alive longer due to veterinary intervention and softer more digestible foods. The increased life span of domestic horses has led to an ever increasing rise in a variety of age-related health problems such as obesity, insulin resistance and laminitis. Cases of colic are also common in older domestic horses, in part due to their worn-out teeth, meaning that they can no longer chew their food properly. Additionally, longer lives mean that cases of arthritis in older horses are not uncommon. This is a point that we should keep in mind because, if an elderly horse is not able to lay down and get up again comfortably, this then leads to sleep deprivation.

It is not uncommon for domestic-living horses to reach their thirties and forties.

Aggressive behaviour differences:

- **Naturally-living horses** usually show very little aggression; particularly with regard to physical contact which could leave one or both parties injured, thus decreasing their chances of survival through predation or starvation. Instead, they use various forms of body language, including lots of gesturing and posturing in order to avoid actual contact. As mentioned previously, some studies have shown that more 'laid back' stallions often produce healthier stronger foals as the foals are not continually being disturbed and can graze and sleep peacefully.

- **Domestic-living horses** may be forced to defend themselves and/or their food. We tend to initiate aggression when we feed concentrates to horses that are kept together. In the natural situation, no -one walks into the herd with buckets of highly desirable, high-energy feed; food is either everywhere or nowhere at any given time. In addition, some domestic horses have little or no social skills due to having been inappropriately managed at some point in their history They may, for example, have been kept separate to other horses, particularly at a formative time in their life and, as a consequence, they may have missed out on learning appropriate social behaviours. These horses can become overly aggressive or can be more easily bullied.

Naturally-living horses use various forms of body language.

Parasite management differences:

- **Naturally-living horses** are able to control parasitic worms by avoiding eating near their own dung. In addition, a variety of animals graze the same areas that they do, so they all benefit from another natural parasitic worm control system; many parasitic worms are 'host specific' and die out when they are picked up by the 'wrong' animal.

- **Domestic-living horses** may be forced to graze badly managed pasture that has high levels of parasitic worms. Domestic horses are often kept on land that is only ever grazed by horses and is actually 'horse-sick'.

As it can be seen, domestic horses have 'unnatural' stresses placed on them including less opportunity to live as part of a stable herd. They usually receive higher energy food, despite having far fewer demands on their energy than naturally-living horses. In fact, many modern domestic horses have a lifestyle that mirrors the lifestyle of many modern humans; not enough exercise and too much 'junk' or processed food. It is therefore not surprising that domestic horses often suffer from both behavioural problems *and* obesity!

—

If you have not thought about it before you now know that there are many important differences between the lifestyle of naturally-living horses and domestic-living horses. The following sections cover some of these subjects in more detail.

—

The herd behaviour of horses

Most people know and acknowledge that horses are herd animals; even people who have nothing to do with horses tend to know this fact, but many people do not completely understand what this entails. The fuller understanding of horse herd and social behaviour we enjoy nowadays means that domestic horse management practices can be designed to incorporate, rather than ignore, these basic but very important facts about horses.

Naturally-living horses usually live in a family group, a band or a small herd, consisting of a stallion, a few mares and their offspring. Occasionally, multi-male bands (with females) are formed. The offspring (fillies and colts) generally leave the family band when they are around two years old (colts usually sooner than fillies) and they join other bands (in the case of fillies) or form 'bachelor groups' (in the case of colts) where they live until they either form a breeding unit with a filly or, alternatively, win a group of mares (or gather some ousted fillies) of their own. Some of these colts and stallions never actually win/gather their own group of fillies/mares and spend their lives in a group with other bachelor stallions.

Most people know and acknowledge that horses are herd animals; even people who have nothing to do with horses tend to know this fact.

These bands, bachelor groups etc. may intermingle; coming together to form a larger herd for part of the day and branch off at other times. This all depends on the terrain, climate, feed availability etc. Generally, the more available feed is, the closer these bands can live together without conflict. In fact, when there are several bands together in a relatively small area, these bands may temporarily merge on a daily basis, particularly when loafing.

When the individual groups are panicked by a possible predator, they also tend to merge and the enlarged group then acts like a 'shoal of fish' in order to confuse the predator and keep the more vulnerable individuals safe within the group. Once normal grazing is resumed, the groups usually revert back to their original smaller bands.

Using their senses

Horses that live in herds get to exercise their senses frequently; they smell each other when greeting and they smell each other's dung in order to gather 'information' about each other. Their highly developed senses of scent and taste are used whilst grazing in order to aid with plant selection. They use their visual and auditory senses to look out and listen for danger. Touch is very important to horses and mutual grooming bouts are frequent. Horses have a very strong fundamental instinct to form attachments to other horses. These attachments are often for life.

Horses that live in herds get to exercise their senses frequently.

Communication

Horses that live in a herd communicate with one another mainly by using body language that consists of subtle signals. An extensive body language system is necessary in any animal species that live in groups and this behaviour is one of the reasons why herd or pack animals are much easier to train than animals that are solitary by nature because they are used to noticing and responding to the behaviour of other members of the group.

Safety in numbers

Living as part of a herd also has other advantages such as 'safety in numbers'. Grazing involves having the head down in the grass, which reduces visibility and, therefore, having more sets of eyes and ears to rely on means that predators can be seen or heard sooner. A horse living alone in the 'wild' would be much more likely to be caught by a predator and would also expend too much nervous energy by having to stay in a permanently alert state. Horses that live in herds can take it in turns to be alert and to rest and therefore, the responsibility of keeping a lookout is shared among herd members.

Horses that live in herds can take it in turns to be alert and to rest and therefore, the responsibility of keeping a lookout is shared among herd members.

Horses are meant to live in herds and naturally-living horses are never alone by choice. These facts drive the behaviour of horses and cause them to do some of the things that can seem irrational to us, such as panic if they get separated from other horses.

Daily 'time-budgets'

The way that domestic horses spend their 'down time'; the very large part of the day when they are not interacting with humans, actually affects how horses behave overall. For example, a horse that is stressed due to inappropriate living conditions may also be difficult to handle, ride and train due to that stress affecting their behaviour. Understanding what horses do (or should do) with their time is essential for good horse management, and good horse management is essential if you are to have a safe, sound and healthy horse.

Many animal species have been studied in their natural environment in order to discover what the 'time-budget' for that particular species is. The term 'timebudget' means the amount of time an animal spends throughout each day and night doing what is necessary to maintain themselves.

Not surprisingly, animals that catch and eat other animals - predators - and *herbivorous* animals that are prey (grazing animals that are caught and eaten) differ from each other in the amount of time that they spend carrying out daily maintenance activities.

The time-budget of most *predators* involves short periods of high activity (to catch and eat prey) and long periods of inactivity (drowsing and sleeping), in order to digest the high calorie/high protein food (meat) that they have eaten. Dogs and cats are typical predators; notice how long it takes your dog or cat to eat their food and then how many hours they sleep.

Horses, being typical herbivores, display very different behaviour to carnivores because they, unlike the meat-eaters, have to be alert most of the time whilst watching and listening for predators. In addition, they have to eat for a much larger part of each day because their food is relatively low in calories and takes a long time to collect and chew.

Horses have one of the longest daily grazing periods of all the plant eating herbivores because they do not ruminate (regurgitate and re-chew their food). As horses chew their food only once, they have to do it very thoroughly. Once swallowed, the food can generally only be broken down further by the various mi-cro-organisms in the gut, so the better the food is chewed before swallowing, the better the micro-organisms can do their job. The horse digests food in the hindgut while grazing. This means that a horse spends most of the day and night 'on the hoof', grazing, ready to flee if necessary.

Studies have shown that the time-budget of adult naturally-living horses comprises of:

- Grazing, between 12-16 hours a day.
- Sleeping, between 2-6 hours a day.
- Loafing, between 2-6 hours a day.

Time spent grazing

Naturally-living horses usually spread their time spent grazing throughout the day and night, with the most intensive grazing periods tending to be at dawn and dusk.

Horses graze in what are termed 'bouts' which are usually between one and a half to three hours long and interspersed with bouts of sleeping and loafing. The grazing bout length is determined partly by how fibrous the pasture is. Older grasses are more, more fibrous and bulky, therefore the grazing bouts are shorter and more frequent (because the horses 'feels fuller' sooner) and on younger, less fibrous pasture the gazing bouts are longer and less frequent (because it takes longer for the horse to 'feel fuller').

The time - budget of horses includes a lot of grazing.

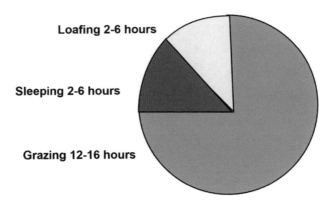

The act of eating is very important to horses because, in the natural situation, grazing takes up more time than all of their other behaviours put together, including sleeping.

The *total* time spent grazing each day depends on the quality of the grass/plants that are available. On better quality/more abundant feed, a horse will spend less time grazing (between 12 and 16 hours in total) and more time loafing (carrying out social behaviours) and sleeping. However, this will still result in a very obese horse if the grass is high in energy.

During hard times, such as drought or a harsh winter, horses will increase their grazing time to up to as much as 20 hours a day (if any plants are available).

Horses are browsers and foragers as well as grazing animals and will eat leaves, twigs and almost anything fibrous, including poisonous plants, if there is nothing else to eat. During these times, loafing behaviour becomes of lower priority and the horse spends all available hours foraging and sleeping.

The ability to increase their total grazing time when necessary is a factor that makes horses such a successful feral animal in tough and varied climates around the world. When the going gets tough, a horse simply increases the amount of time spent eating, and therefore increases the amount of food eaten if any food is available. Even though this food may be very low quality, as it would be in times of drought or cold harsh weather, it still means that the horse usually manages to survive because of the increased volume of food consumed.

In tough conditions when their feed source becomes more fibrous or lower in quality, this strategy makes horses more successful than certain other animals, such as cattle. A horse's digestive system has evolved to allow them to survive in very harsh conditions indeed (see the section ***The grazing behaviour of horses***).

The total time spent grazing each day depends on the quality of the grass/plants that are available.

Interestingly, if a horse is removed from pasture for a few hours; a management tactic often carried out by horse-owners with the intention of reducing an overweight horse's pasture intake, the horse will condense their grazing time into this shorter time period when they are turned out again by simultaneously increasing their bite and chew rate. So, for example, if a horse is confined to a yard or stable for several hours and then turned out again, it will not make much, if any, difference to their total intake for the day!

Horses are browsers and foragers as well as grazing animals and will eat leaves, twigs and almost anything fibrous, including poisonous plants, if there is nothing else to eat.

Time spent sleeping

Adult horses usually sleep/doze for a total of about 4 hours per 24 hours (young horses sleep for longer). These four hours are divided roughly into totals of two hours spent sleeping lying down and two hours spent dozing standing up.

Like grazing, sleeping takes place in bouts. A sleeping bout is around 15 minutes at a time and is interspersed with grazing and loafing bouts. For example, a horse might sleep lying down for 15 minutes and then graze some more, then lay down to sleep again and so on.

Horses have various sleeping/dozing positions - lying flat out on the side with the head and neck outstretched, lying down but resting on the sternum (with the nose resting on the ground or with the head up off the ground) or a third position, which involves the horse dozing standing up. A horse uses what is termed 'the stay apparatus' to lock the joints of the legs in place, and can even do this while resting one of its hind legs when nodding off in the standing position.

Horses use a lot of energy when sleeping flat out on their side due to having large lungs. Lying down rests the legs but these large lungs (and other organs) then have to work harder when a horse is stretched out flat and this is why a horse will often make a groaning noise when fully prone, as breathing is quite an effort in this position. However, this sleeping position is essential as it is thought to be the only position in which a horse can achieve deep (REM, rapid eye movement) sleep.

Horses use a lot of energy when sleeping flat out on their side due to having large lungs.

Resting/sleeping on the sternum is a compromise position, the horse is able to sleep deeper than when standing, and rest all four legs, but cannot sleep as deeply as they can in the fully prone position.

As horses age, they find getting down and up again from the ground more difficult and, eventually, they may stop lying down altogether because they have learned that it is too difficult to get back up again. To a horse, being able to get up from the ground quickly is an essential survival factor. Horses innately know that they have to be able to rise quickly and run from danger. Be aware of this with old (especially if arthritic) horses because they may not be getting enough (or any) deep (REM) sleep due to having stiff, sore joints and this can therefore become a welfare issue. This is one of the factors that should help you to make a decision about if and when to euthanise an old horse.

In a group of horses, one horse usually stays standing when the others are asleep on the ground and this standing horse is more alert than the others, even if dozing, while the others sleep more deeply. This is a good example of how herds operate; horses that live alone do not get to benefit from this strategy of shared responsibility. Some nervous horses are even unwilling to lie down frequently enough when on their own as they have no other horse to watch over them as they sleep. These horses can suffer from sleep deprivation as they are unwilling to spend enough, or indeed any, time sleeping in the fully recumbent position.

In a group of horses, one horse usually stays standing when the others are asleep on the ground.

Time spent loafing

The term 'loafing' encompasses all the other behaviours that horses carry out during the day and night. Loafing includes activities such as mutual grooming (allo-grooming) and playing and even includes time spent simply standing around together, especially in the shade when it is hot, nose to tail. They use their tails to keep flies off each other; a form of 'you scratch my back and I'll scratch yours' behaviour. In cold, wet weather, horses will stand in a sheltered spot together because their large bodies help to keep each other warm.

Standing around together is of top priority to horses, they will often disregard other comforts in order to be able to stand next to each other. This is demonstrated when horses are kept separately in 'private paddocks' where they will ignore shade/shelter in order to stand next to each other on either side of the fence.

Mutual grooming involves two horses approaching each other and using their incisor teeth to 'groom' each other in another example of a mutually beneficial behaviour. Mutual grooming is a very important behaviour for horses. Areas that they cannot reach with their own teeth can be scratched by the other horse and it is also a way of maintaining bonds among herd members. Studies have shown that, during bouts of mutual grooming, the heart rate of a horse is significantly lowered.

'You scratch my back and I'll scratch yours'.

Playing is also very important to horses of all ages. In young horses, play is an opportunity to learn and practice the skills required for adult life. Younger horses spend more time than older horses playing, but all horses naturally play even into old age if they are able (in contrast to many other large grazing herbivores). Horses will play with other horses, in the case of domestic horses, geldings (castrated males) play together as if they are 'wild' colts. Horses will also play with objects such as sticks and, in the domestic situation; they will play with other objects such as road cones, 'horse balls' etc.

A herd of normal, healthy horses will get excited and tend to run around at certain times such as when turned out into a new pasture or when the sun comes out after a period of rain. Sometimes no excuse is required and horses will gallop 'just for the fun of it'. When horses are deprived of the company of other horses, they are deprived of the opportunity to play with other horses.

This active behaviour is partly due to the fact that horses, in a natural situation, have to be ready to flee from a predator instantly. The first line of defence for a horse is to run, therefore horses 'practice' fleeing as part of their natural behaviour. In contrast cattle use their horns to defend themselves and their young so running away is only one part of their escaping predation.

The grazing behaviour of horses

Compared to a meat-eater, the natural food of horses is low in calories and takes a long time to collect, chew and digest. Horses are herbivores; this means that, like other herbivores, they eat plants and lots of them.

Horses are not ruminants

Their physiology however is different to that of many other grazing herbivores in that they are *not* ruminants (like cattle and sheep). Horses eat relatively *more* food but digest it *less* efficiently than most ruminants. Because of this fact, horses spend *more time* grazing than cattle and sheep and they *ferment* their food in the hind-gut while grazing. Ruminants spend time ruminating (regurgitating and re-chewing their food) *as well* as grazing.

Put another way, horses *eat more* but invest *less time* on each mouthful of food, ruminants *eat less* but invest *more time* on each mouthful of food.

This strategy means that horses are more successful in very tough conditions when their feed source becomes more fibrous or lower in nutritional quality. A horse's digestive system has evolved to allow them to survive in very harsh conditions.

Horses are not ruminants.

The importance of fibre to horses

Acid continuously builds up in the stomach of a horse. A naturally-living horse has access to fibre most, if not all of the time (even when this fibre is very poor quality and low in energy, such as leaves and even twigs). This means that a naturally-living horse can nearly always find something fibrous to eat and so the acid in the stomach is usually buffered by the saliva that the horse swallows while chewing. An important point here is that in horses saliva flows in response to food in the mouth. If domestic horses do not have access to enough fibre, and therefore they are not chewing and swallowing enough saliva, this acid reaches critical levels in the stomach and causes gastric ulcers.

Not getting enough fibre is also one reason why domestic horses will sometimes eat poisonous plants, strip the bark from trees or chew fences. Indeed a horse will eat almost anything rather than allow the painful gastric acid to build up in their stomach. For this reason 'starving' even a fat horse is not the right way to go about managing weight (more about this later).

Not getting enough fibre is also one reason why domestic horses will sometimes eat poisonous plants, strip the bark from trees....

Food selection in horses

When moving around the home-range, the horses often move in single file to make it easier to travel over the terrain, however, once they begin grazing, the band spreads itself out, searching for and selecting a wide variety of plant species.

Grass is their main staple although they will eat other plants including certain bushes and trees. Horses will even eat berries and other fruits if they get the chance. The naturally living horse's diet is much more varied than that of a domestic horse. Naturally-living horses are thought to eat as many as 100 different species of plant throughout the year. Their diet is not balanced daily, but it becomes a balanced diet throughout the year as different plants are available to be eaten. Each plant they eat over the year provides the horse with different minerals and nutrients on an *annual* basis.

It is therefore important that you aim to have a variety of species in your pasture and to ensure that your pasture is not a monoculture (a monoculture is where there is only one species of plant in a given area). A good pasture for horses contains plants such as legumes, herbs, sedges etc. *as well* as several species of grass.

—

For more information see the second book in this series *The Equicentral System Series Book 2 - Healthy Land, Healthy Pasture, Healthy Horses.*

—

Selective grazing habits of horses

Horses are highly selective grazers. They are able to be much more selective than cows for example because their prehensile (highly flexible) top lip allows them to sort what they want from what they do not want as they graze. They also have two sets of incisors which meet and are very sharp. The sharp, paired incisors of horses allow them to bite plants down to ground level. Horses, if left on a pasture for too long, will continuously select plants that they like and graze them to the ground, leaving the rest to grow long and rank. The long, rank areas are also where they drop their dung (see the section *The 'dunging behaviour' of domestic horses*). The types of plants that horses prefer eventually become grazed out unless particularly hardy.

Once they begin grazing, the band spreads itself out, searching for and selecting a wide variety of plant species.

Horses have no concept of 'leaving some for another day' or any other grazing management strategies that would result in more grass in the future. If grass is available horses will eat it, even if they make themselves incredibly fat in the process or if they completely eat out their favoured species.

Chewing behaviour of horses

As horses have evolved to eat for many hours at a time, they have huge muscles in the jaw which enable chewing for hour after hour. When you are feeding your horse/s, remember that they are meant to eat large amounts of low-energy fibrous food (the equivalent of vegetables and salad to us), not small amounts, or even worse, large amounts of high-energy food (the equivalent of 'junk food' to us). Low-energy, fibrous food takes a long time to chew and digest and keeps a horse occupied (and fulfils the chewing need) for hours at a time.

Chewing is important for the production of saliva that buffers acid in the stomach and helps to keep stomach ulcers at bay. While chewing, a horse is relaxed whilst, conversely, a horse that becomes alert stops chewing. This is because chewing is noisy and it is only by stopping chewing that the horse can hear properly.

Their prehensile (highly flexible) top lip allows them to sort what they want from what they do not want as they graze.

Head position while grazing

The head of a horse is in a lowered position when eating plants (as opposed to eating out of a raised feeder for example). The joints and soft tissues of the horse's head and neck have evolved so that the head can comfortably be kept low for hours at a time; interspersed with occasional periods of lifting the head to look around. Whilst in this head-down position, the horse is relatively relaxed.

This lowered head position also serves another function; to drain the airways. The lungs of a horse are large and delicate and, whenever the head of a horse is lowered, the airways are draining debris down the nose, helping to keep the lungs clean.

The head of a horse is in a lowered position when eating plants.

Walking while grazing

While a horse is grazing, they are also walking because the plants are stationary and the horse has to keep moving in order to graze them. A horse generally only bites each plant once or twice before selecting another plant (if the pasture is healthy, not too short and is biodiverse). It is estimated that a horse takes 10,000 steps a day while grazing and, if a horse walks/grazes at 1mph or 2kmph, this means that they will cover approximately 12miles or 24km each day! This slow, steady movement is vital for horse health. The circulatory system of a horse depends on this movement to keep blood and lymphatic fluid moving around the body; not to mention the many other advantages of exercise. Horses that are kept mainly confined miss out on the numerous benefits of grazing.

'Overeating' in horses

Deliberate 'overeating' in horses is due to an innate need that drives them to eat more than is needed when food is available and to store it as body fat. Most mammals have developed this strategy to get them through hard times. In the natural situation, this is offset by reduced nutrition in times of scarcity e.g. winter or drought.

'Overeating' in naturally-living horses

The type of food available to naturally-living horses means that this increase in body fat is usually reasonably gradual. Then, when feed is not so readily available (such as during a harsh winter or drought),reserves of body fat can be utilised for survival.

In an ideal year, naturally-living horses will enter winter slightly overweight, lose condition over the winter (as they use up those body fat reserves) and enter spring slightly underweight, when the rich high-sugar grasses start to re-grow. This means that they have some 'lee way' with regards eating the higher-energy spring grasses.

'Overeating' in domestic horses

This seasonal weight fluctuation is rarely seen in domestic horses because they are usually fed supplementary feed as soon as the pasture loses nutrition. This can have health implications, particularly in regard to obesity and its associated conditions. In the domestic situation, a horse will still attempt to *always* put on weight whenever possible (eating lots during times of food plenty is a survival strategy). Our modern horses do not reason that food is continuously provided by their owner, nor will they be particularly bothered by being overweight.

A further complication is that it is when horses are deprived of food in an attempt to force them to lose weight, they go into 'starvation mode'. This can actually increase insulin resistance levels and can cause them to 'gorge' whenever they get the opportunity.

A certain amount of insulin resistance occurs naturally in horses; it allows them to gain weight over spring/summer. However, if these levels are allowed to remain high, then problems occur and the horse then lays down too much fat. Domestic horses tend to be fed too much over the winter months, not allowing these insulin resistance levels to regulate themselves.

As the fat level increases it can secrete chemicals known as Cytokines, which have an effect on the brain and change the way the body responds to another type of chemical known as Leptin. Leptin is an appetite regulator, but once the brain fails to respond to it, the horse continues to overeat, entering into a vicious circle. In the domestic situation, a horse should actually have constant access to food, but that food should be low in calories, so that this gorging behaviour is not triggered.

When winter comes, the horse should not be automatically rugged and fed more food but instead, this period should be seen as the best time to reduce weight in a natural way (in overweight horses).

In the domestic situation, a horse will still attempt to always put on weight whenever possible.

Domestic horses must, of course, be regularly monitored for increases and decreases in condition. As a horse owner, you need to be aware of what is considered a dangerous level of weight increase because this can lead to life threatening conditions such as laminitis. At the same time, you need to be aware of what constitutes reasonable weight loss.

Modern day horse management has resulted in many horses being over confined, under worked and fed meals that are too high in energy and too low in fibre. These types of feed are eaten much more quickly (due to being more energy dense and less bulky) and this results in long periods of time where the horse has nothing to do.

An additional problem is that modern grasses are largely developed for the cattle and sheep industries, with these grasses increasingly being bred to be higher in sugar and starch as this is what farmers need and want for milk or meat production. In most countries (those that have temperate rather than tropical climates), improved ryegrass has become the number one grass of choice for farmers. Horse owners need to be very aware that for sedentary domestic horses and most of them fall into this category, this grass is far too high in energy.

A study has shown that large numbers (possibly over 50%) of domestic horses in the UK, for example, are obese. The same study showed that most owners tended to underestimate the condition score of their overweight horses by at least one point on the condition scoring scale. The subject of obesity in domestic horses is becoming a major welfare issue.

Incorrect feed types and amounts can cause problems, either behavioural, physiological, or both (see the sections **Abnormal horse behaviour** and **Common physiological disorders in horses**).

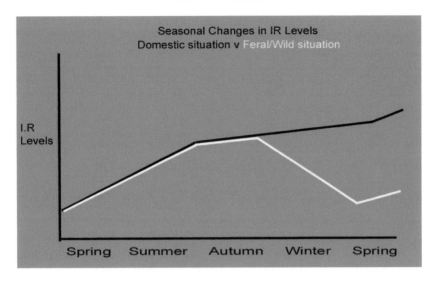

Unfortunately, current practice for the management of overweight/laminitic horses is commonly to restrict their food and this usually involves restricting their movement because they are removed from pasture. Try to keep in mind with horses (even overweight ones) that you should **not be aiming to feed less food but that you should be aiming to feed food that is lower in calories;** the equivalent of less chocolate and more salad to us. **Starving even a fat horse is cruel and counterproductive**. An additional factor for horses, much like with humans that are overweight, is that they are often not receiving enough exercise.

Modern day horse management has resulted in many horses being over confined, under worked and fed meals that are too high in energy and too low in fibre.

Exercise/movement (as long as a horse is not in pain) should be seen as **one of the most important factors** in the management of horses. Horses are meant to move a lot on a daily basis and the main reason we are seeing so many problems with horses today is the same reason why similar problems are on the rise in humans (type 2 diabetes etc.) – inactivity coupled with food that is too high in energy. People who are diagnosed with such conditions are given the advice that they must eat the right kinds of food and **exercise**. The same is true for horses, so locking them up in a stable without exercise or enough high fibre food is not good management (see the section *Ideas for extra exercise*).

The pastured behaviour of domestic horses

Horses are generally regarded as being 'bad' for the land, but this is actually not true. Horses, like all grazing animals, are excellent for the land when allowed to carry out their natural behaviours and it is for this reason that, in many areas of the world, they are being used for the purpose of 'conservation grazing'. However, they *will* cause damage when they are allowed to *overgraze* land, simply because there are too many horses for the amount of land available, or they have been kept on a given area of land for too long. This damage can be alleviated by careful management.

Locking horses up in a stable without exercise or enough high fibre food is not good management - note the marks on the wall from stereotypic 'head-swinging' behaviour.

When horses are kept as domestic animals, we have to acknowledge their natural behaviour, but we also have to manage them so that they do not overgraze pasture. By allowing horses to overgraze, we set up problems for the future which results in less and less pasture over time; the grasses become stressed (and therefore more dangerous to graze) and the number of pasture species diminish which also creates a loss of biodiversity and has negative effects on the environment, such as soil loss and water pollution.

The way that horses behave when turned out in a paddock warrants consideration because it affects their management *and* land management. The negative aspects outlined in this section can all be mitigated with better management and this will be explained later in this publication, but this section describes what *commonly* occurs on land where horses are kept. Once you are more aware of the damage that horses *can* cause to the land, you will be more motivated to make changes. Horses can cause a lot of wear and tear to land and this is due to a combination of factors. Damage to pasture is caused not only by overgrazing, but also the 'standing around behaviour' that horses carry out when not actually grazing, and by the 'tracking' caused by horses. High activity will also cause problems in some situations.

Horses, like all grazing animals, are excellent for the land when allowed to carry out their natural behaviours and it is for this reason that, in many areas of the world, they are being used for the purpose of 'conservation grazing' - Wicken Fen UK.

The 'standing around' behaviour of domestic horses

Horses will stand around (loaf), sometimes for hours at a time, for various reasons. Horses graze in 'bouts' (see the section *Time spent grazing*) and when a grazing bout has finished they carry out other behaviours for a period of time, until it is time to start another grazing bout. These other behaviours include snoozing/sleeping, playing and just simply 'loafing' (see the section *Daily 'time-budgets'*). Standing around after a grazing bout is perfectly natural behaviour but horses will increase their time spent standing in certain situations. Horses often have a favourite 'hang out' area such as somewhere that is shady/sheltered, near resources such as water, a high flat area or, most often, this spot is near the gateway.

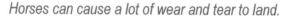

Horses can cause a lot of wear and tear to land.

Factors that increase 'standing around' behaviour

- When they are turned out on bare (overgrazed 'pasture'). Grazing and walking are linked behaviours and so if there is no pasture to eat they will simply stand around (once they have run off any excess energy).

- When turned out on pasture that is a monoculture horses soon realise that there are only one or two types of plant to eat and they reduce their time spent seeking out variety and overgraze the area near their favourite loafing area. They also increase their time spent standing.

- Horses that are being fed supplementary feed will stand around (usually at a gateway) even if there is plenty of pasture available and wait, long before feed

76

time. The *anticipation* of concentrate feed causes horses to reduce their grazing bout time and increase their time spent standing.

Horses that are being fed supplementary feed will stand around (usually at a gateway) even if there is plenty of pasture available

Good land management involves removing this 'pressure' whenever possible because it causes many land management issues which result in bare/compacted soil, mud, dust and weeds etc. Fences and gates *prevent* horses from being able to move themselves to where they want/need to be, so they have no choice but to stand for hours at a gate or under tree.

It makes no difference to a horse where they carry out these behaviours, so they may as well carry them out in an area that is designed to cope with this pressure so that the pasture can rest and recuperate. Whenever horses are not grazing, they should carry out all other behaviours in an area that is created for that purpose and they should preferably *be able to take themselves* to that area. That area needs to contain all the elements that attract the horses to spend time there such as water, shade/shelter etc. See the section **The Equicentral System** for information about how you encourage horses to *voluntarily* eliminate this pressure on the land.

The 'gateway behaviour' of domestic horses

Very high use areas on a horse property include the gateways. Therefore they are often the most degraded area in a paddock. The land just inside a gateway is often bare and has compacted soil. It will also tend to be dusty or muddy (depending on the weather conditions) and this bare area is often immediately surrounded by weeds (the area immediately near the gate is usually too degraded even for weeds to grow). The area just beyond that is often the most heavily grazed as horses spend a great deal of their time around gateways.

*Whenever horses are not grazing, they should carry out all other behaviours in an area that is created for that purpose and they should preferably **be able to take themselves** to that area.*

One of the main reasons that horses stand in gateways is that owners arrive here at feed times – either with feed, or to lead them to where the feed is. In most cases in a domestic situation, we have to provide supplementary feed to horses, at least at certain times of the year. It is important to understand that the very first time we provide feed for our horses, their behaviour begins to change.

—

We are not for a moment suggesting that providing additional feed for your horse/s is a bad thing. We are simply pointing out how supplementing the diet is linked with land management problems. Anticipation of food causes horses to spend less time grazing and more time hanging around the gate area, sometimes for several hours, looking out for this feed (or for you coming to take them to the feed).

—

This hanging around behaviour adds to the already heavy use of the gateway area, causing more soil compaction, dust, mud and weeds. More dung is also dropped in this area, adding to the muddy 'soup' when the weather is wet. This means that horses may be standing for hours in filthy muddy conditions and it is therefore not surprising that horses in this situation are prone to mud fever – a fungal/bacterial skin condition caused by mud.

In the naturally-living situation, horses would never stand for hours in mud, instead, they would take themselves to a higher, drier area. Also, of course, no-one brings a pile of highly palatable food to the same spot everyday either.

Another factor to consider with gateways is that they are one of the most dangerous areas on a horse property for both horses *and* humans. Anxious horses milling around in wet, slippery conditions is dangerous enough, even before you add humans and the potential of food to the mix.

Gateways are often the most degraded area in a paddock.

—

See the third book in this series *The Equicentral System Series Book 3 – Horse Property Planning and Development* for more information about gateways and how to make them safer.

—

The 'tracking behaviour' of domestic horses

Grazing animals create 'tracks' in areas that they frequently travel. In addition to the land management issues outlined above, these tracks cause erosion because they provide a pathway in which water is able to move faster. This faster-moving water causes erosion, which then creates a vicious circle of events as it removes more soil, creates a deeper channel and so on. **Horses create these tracks in the following situations:**

- A separated horse will walk a fence line to try and get to other horses. In this case, this behaviour could also eventually undermine a fence as the ever deepening track cuts in to the soil that is holding the fence posts in the ground. Separated stallions, in particular, will carry out this behaviour.

- Horses will create tracks between areas that they frequent such as a water trough and a shade/shelter or favourite loafing area.

The active behaviour of domestic horses

Healthy horses will often canter or gallop on pasture. This is normal behaviour for a horse as long as it is not caused by anxiety as a horse tries to get to other horses. Horses are naturally much more active animals than cattle for example, who defend first and run second. Remember, horses are primarily flight animals, so running around is actually practising this behaviour. This active behaviour when turned out is increased when horses are confined for long periods and when they are fed high levels of concentrate feeds. This active behaviour does not cause harm to the land as long as there is a good covering of plants. It does cause damage if the land is extremely dry or is wet.

Grazing animals create 'tracks' in areas that they frequently travel.

An issue that can occur with pastured horses that, whilst not detrimental to land management, *is* detrimental to their safety, is that of horses playing/socialising with other horses over a fence. In particular, separated horses will play with other horses over an adjoining fence. This is *extremely dangerous behaviour;* fence injuries are very high on the list of serious, expensive and possibly life threatening injuries to horses). Good safe horse management entails ensuring that horses *never* play over a fence.

A separated horse will walk a fence line causing soil erosion.

The 'dunging behaviour' of domestic horses

The 'dunging behaviour' of horses is similar to that of other grazing herbivores in that they avoid grazing near any dung piles from their own species, but will graze near that of other species. So, for example, a horse will not graze close to a pile of horse manure but will graze near a cow pat. This is thought to be an innate parasitic worm avoidance strategy.

In addition, horses 'group' their dung in to areas within a pasture (the 'roughs') and graze in others (the 'lawns') this can lead to a situation sometimes termed a 'horse-sick' pasture (see the section *'Horse-sick' pasture*). In contrast, cows and sheep are not as rigid as to where they drop dung in a pasture.

Healthy horses will often canter or gallop on pasture. This is normal behaviour for a horse as long as it is not caused by anxiety as a horse tries to get to other horses.

In a naturally-living situation, horses are not forced to graze over their own manure due to the space that they have available to them. In such a situation, many different species of animal graze the same areas, each grazing near and around each other's manure and taking in each other's parasitic worms which kills the parasites.

'Horse-sick' pasture

Pastures that have well-marked areas of roughs and lawns are often termed 'horse-sick'. An old fashioned but still used term that generally means that the land has a high level of parasitic worms *and* has well-established roughs and lawns.

Horse 'dunging behaviour' leads to:

- **Progressively less grazing each year** as the ever decreasing lawn areas usually have to provide feed for at least the same amount of horses as the previous year. Without intervention, more and more of the pasture becomes unavailable for grazing over time.

- **An imbalance of nutrients** as horses take from the lawns, by grazing and deposit manure in the roughs. Horse manure is high in nutrients such as nitrogen and, therefore, the roughs receive lots of fertiliser and the lawns do not.

- **A higher number of parasitic worms** on the land because the manure is not being managed properly e.g. picked up on smaller paddocks or harrowed-in on larger paddocks. The number of infective parasite larvae in roughs is many times greater than in the lawns, but these infective larvae do migrate to the lawns, particularly after rainfall, meaning that horses are then infected by them.

- **Monocultures of short, stressed grass and roughs** which contain only long, rank, inedible plants and weeds; especially the types of weeds that thrive on high levels of nutrients. These areas become a 'seed bank' for weeds as the seeds build up and are either deposited in the soil within the rough, or blow across and 'infect' the lawns.

- **A poor impression** because horse-sick land is unsightly and gives the general public a negative view of horsekeeping.

Horse 'dunging behaviour', therefore, is something that has to be managed in the domestic situation otherwise horses will render a pasture horse-sick and increase their parasitic worm burden.

'Horse-sick' pasture.

—

See the second book in this series ***The Equicentral System Series Book 2 - Healthy Land, Healthy Pasture, Healthy Horses*** for more information about this subject.

—

Recognising stress in domestic horses

It is sometimes difficult to know if a horse is stressed, particularly because many horse owners do not know what signs to look for. One problem is that horses do not outwardly show signs of stress in the same way that certain other animals do. Horses do not naturally squeal or make any other vocalisation to signal pain. This is because a prey animal, such as a horse, is unwilling to signal that they are in pain for fear that they will be seen as being vulnerable and therefore more likely to be singled out by a predator.

If a domestic horse is in pain e.g. is lame or has been struck with a whip, it does not make a sound. This seemingly compliant behaviour extends to when a horse is stressed. Think about how dogs in cages, such as those in an animal shelter, usually make it clear that they do not want to be there by barking, whining and jumping up at the cage front. Such behaviour differs hugely from the way horses react when similarly over-confined, for example when fully-stabled, who generally make no sound to signal that they would rather not be restrained. This may be mistaken by humans to mean that the horse is 'happy' with the situation.

Horses do not outwardly show signs of stress in the same way that certain other animals do. Horses do not naturally squeal or make any other vocalisation to signal pain.

Horse owners need to understand that, by restricting natural behaviours, we are creating stresses in horses. It is virtually impossible to create an environment where a domestic horse is kept fully naturally, and there has to be compromises in order for horses to be kept in captivity, but it is important that the choices we make do not cause stress to horses.

Abnormal horse behaviour

Animals in captivity (domestic and captive wild animals) are less stressed if important facts about their physiology and behaviour are taken into account when designing and implementing management systems for them. As already mentioned, most modern zoos in the western world have taken these facts on board and go to great lengths to enrich the lifestyle of any animals in their care by providing better, and usually bigger, enclosures and more natural feeding experiences for them. They also, if it is appropriate to the species in question, group house them, rather than keep them separately as used to be common with zoo animals.

Domestic horses are no different; they become stressed and can develop abnormal behaviours if they are not allowed to carry out certain natural behaviours. For example, living as part of a herd, playing, mutual grooming and grazing are all part of their natural range of behaviours.

Domestic horses become stressed and can develop abnormal behaviours if they are not allowed to carry out certain natural behaviours.

Stereotypic behaviours are not seen in animals in the wild and are therefore understood to be abnormal and as being a negative factor in the management of animals in captivity. Naturally-living horses do not exhibit these stereotypic behaviours because they are not subjected to the same stresses as domestic horses, have a natural diet and also have a complex and varied lifestyle.

Stereotypic behaviours can occur in all animals, including humans, in which case they are often called 'obsessive compulsive' behaviours - compulsive hand washing is one example. Be aware though that just because a horse is not showing such behaviours does *not* mean that they are *not* stressed. Some horses, rather than developing stereotypic behaviours, develop 'learned helplessness' (see the section **Naturally-living v domestic-living horses**).

In horses, stereotypic behaviours take various forms and the most common ones are listed below (but there are actually many more):

- Fence-walking. Repeatedly walking backwards and forwards along a fence line.

- Weaving. Repeatedly rocking from one front leg to the other in a stable or at a gate, some horses will also do this when travelling.

- Crib-biting. Grasping an object (an old fashioned name for a horse's feed manger is a crib) with the front teeth (incisors) and swallowing.

Fence-walking - repeatedly walking backwards and forwards along a fence.

- Wind-sucking. Arching the neck and swallowing without grasping an object.

- Box-walking. Repeatedly pacing around and around a stable.

- Wall-kicking. Repeatedly kicking the walls of a stable, usually with one or both back feet, even to the point of making themselves sore/lame.

- Self-mutilation. Swinging the head to repeatedly bite themselves. This behaviour is typically carried out by stallions.

In the horse world, stereotypic behaviours are inaccurately and unfortunately termed 'vices'. This leads to the assumption that the horse is 'misbehaving' and has to be restrained or punished, rather than recognising that the horse is simply reacting to stress.

Horses which have 'vices' are then often put under even more stress in an attempt to *prevent* them from carrying out these behaviours (by using windsucking collars and anti-weaving bars for example).

Much of the information that is readily available to horse owners on the subject of stereotypic behaviours, for example in magazines or on the Internet is archaic and even cruel. This information usually only concentrates on prevention methods and does nothing to reduce the stress levels of the horse in question; in fact, they usually vastly increase stress levels for the horse.

There are also many products on the market that attempt to physically prevent horses from carrying out stereotypic behaviours and these products, such as crib biting/wind-sucking collars, again do not treat the cause of the problem and can in fact increase the stress felt by the horse. Prevention is not the answer, as it simply increases the stress levels and does nothing to make the behaviour disappear. In practice, these measures will usually make the behaviour more likely to occur once the preventative device has been removed. This is why horses that wear a 'cribbing/sucking' collar usually begin to crib/suck immediately the collar is removed, which makes their owner feel justified for using it.

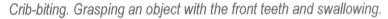

Crib-biting. Grasping an object with the front teeth and swallowing.

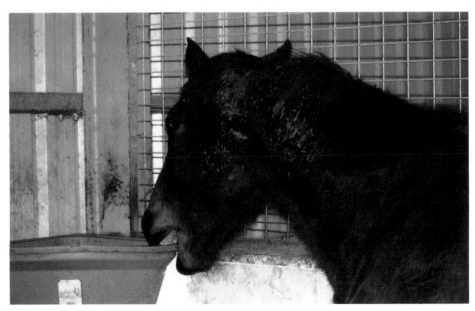

The stereotypic behaviour is the horse's way of coping with the stress and gadgets which stop the horse from carrying out this behaviour simply mask the symptoms. This suppressed behaviour may then manifest in a different abnormal behaviour, such as 'learned helplessness' or even aggression.

Sometimes it is helpful to put things into context by taking things which might seem innocuous in one situation and imagining them in another situation to compare them. Imagine visiting a zoo and observing animals wearing preventative devices of some kind. You would *not* be happy about the situation and would probably complain, yet in many stables you will see various preventative devices such as crib-biting/wind-sucking collars and weaving bars commonly being used. A relatively new invention is an electric collar for horses that crib-bite and wind-suck! This collar delivers a small electric shock to the horse if the horse attempts to tense the muscles in the throat area (a prerequisite for cribbing/sucking). Such a device would never be allowed in a zoo where the animals are on public display because the public would find it totally unacceptable.

Preventative methods do nothing to reduce the stress levels of the horse.

Oral stereotypic behaviours such as crib-biting and wind-sucking can arise because the horse does not have access to enough fibre. When horses chew, they also produce and swallow saliva in copious amounts. Research has shown that horses that crib-bite and wind-suck are actually swallowing saliva to relieve pain in the stomach by buffering the acid in the stomach. It used to be thought that they were swallowing air, hence the term 'wind-sucking'. Other stereotypic behaviours such as weaving and box/fence-walking are due to frustration at not being able to move enough or move towards where they want to be; usually to be near other horses.

There are many outdated myths connected with stereotypic behaviours; for example, it is commonly believed that if a horse watches another horse performing a stereotypic behaviour, they will learn to do it. This is called observational learning and does not apply here. Horses do not learn in this way once they are adults. If more than one horse is exhibiting a stereotypic behaviour in a given area, it is more likely to be because both or all of the horses are living in conditions that cause these stereotypic behaviours, rather than that they are simply copying each other's behaviour. Isolating horses because of this belief will simply lead to elevated stress and an increase in the behaviour.

It is common to see various preventative devices such as crib-biting/wind-sucking collars being used.

Once a horse has developed the habit of performing a certain stereotypic behaviour it will usually carry on performing the behaviour for the rest of its life, even if the reason the horse was stressed in the first place is removed. The behaviour may be seen much less over time, however, and allowing the horse to perform the behaviour rather than trying to prevent it, whilst at the same time improving the lifestyle of the horse, is usually the best solution (see the section **Enrichment for domestic horses**).

Common physiological disorders in horses

Some of the most important physiological disorders associated with poor management practices that can occur with horses are colic, gastric ulcers, laminitis and insulin resistance.

Colic is a common and potentially deadly condition in horses. Colic is a term used to describe a variety of gastro intestinal disorders in horses that range from mild to very severe. It is probably the number one killer of domestic horses.

Gastric ulcers are a very common occurrence in domestic horses due to the way that they are often managed (on a diet that is too low in fibre).

Laminitis is one of the most serious, crippling diseases of equines. Severe and recurring cases of laminitis can result in the horse being destroyed to prevent further suffering. It is a painful inflammatory condition of the tissues (laminae) that bond the hoof wall to the pedal (coffin) bone in the horses hoof. Its cause is not fully understood, but it is typically associated with incorrect feeding practices. Laminitis can occur when horses are eating too much high sugar/high starch grass or being fed too many concentrates, but not enough low energy fibre. It can also occur when horses are kept on restrictive diets, eating short stressed grass with permanently elevated insulin resistance levels.

Colic, excessive rolling can be a reaction.

Insulin resistance occurs when insulin levels are sufficiently high over a prolonged period of time causing the body's own sensitivity to the hormone to be reduced. Once the body starts to become resistant to insulin, it can be a difficult process to reverse because of the knock on effect of insulin resistance. Higher circulating levels of insulin in the blood stream and weight gain help to further advance insulin resistance.

—

See the **Equiculture website Horse care and welfare page** for links to much more information about the above conditions **www.equiculture.com.au/horse-care-and-welfare.html**

—

Why horses need other horses

One of the most important factors affecting a horse's well-being is to be with other horses. **Some of the various reasons for this are summarised below:**

- **For insect control** – horses need other horses so that they stand head to tail and swish flies out of each others' faces.

- **For sleeping** – horses need other horses so that they can relax enough to sleep. They take it in turns to stand over the others in the herd so that the rest of the herd can lie down and sleep deeply.

- **For mutual grooming** – horses need other horses for the purpose of mutual grooming; something they do this frequently if allowed. Isolated horses and horses wearing rugs cannot do this.

- **For general companionship** – horses have a need for the company of other horses.

- **For eating** – horses eat better in the presence of other horses. They need other horses to feel safe enough to eat properly, because their head is down in the grass when grazing, they feel more secure when there are more eyes and ears to look out for danger.

- **To feel safe and reduce stress** – horses need other horses for all of the above so that they feel safer and less stressed.

- **For exercise** – horses move more when they are with other horses. They move to keep up with the others if the others decide to move and they play with each other.

Reasons for separating horses

Horse owners often separate horses for the following myths/reasons:

- **So that they are easier to supplementary feed** – it is generally a good idea to separate horses *just for the period* that it takes a horse to eat any supplementary feed they may be receiving, because supplementary feed causes high levels of competition and therefore aggression (see the section ***Naturally-living v do-mestic-living horses***). However, *it is not fair* to keep a horse separate to others horses 24/7 *just* because this makes it easier for an owner to feed their horse. This means that the horse has to forego socialising with other horses all day, simply to make things easier for the owner during the small part of the day when the horse is being supplementary fed.

Horses need other horses for various reasons and functions.

- **To keep them safer** – horse owners often believe that separated horses are safer but, in actual fact, fence injuries often cause more damage than other horses do and horses are far more likely to come into contact with a fence when they are separated from other horses, than when they are kept in herds, because isolated horses are constantly trying to get back to other horses. For example, the strong instinct horses have to be together means that separated horses will 'walk the fence' or even go through or over a fence or gate to be with another horse. The resultant fence injuries are usually far worse than anything that horses do to each other when kept together. Additionally, in an ill-advised attempt to prevent physical damage, untold mental damage is being caused by keeping them in 'solitary confinement'. Herd living is an important part of the socialisation of a horse, and research is being carried out into how important this is in terms of a horse's learning development.

- **Because that is the rule where they keep them** – unfortunately this is often the case and is becoming more so. 'Private' paddocks are now regarded as a plus point at livery yards and horse owners, not always understanding what horses really need, tend to seek out such places. However, there *are* forward thinking and successful livery yards that are going against this trend.

- **Because their horse does not like other horses** – when horses have been separated from other horses they can lose their 'socialisation skills'. In particular, if horses are separated when very young, as is often the case with valuable race horses and other competition horses, for example, they lose out on the important lessons that older herd members would have taught them.

Most horses can still be integrated into a herd later in life, but occasionally some cannot (see the section *Introducing horses to herd living*). In many cases horse owners are afraid to integrate horses and this can simply be the owner over-reacting to the initial noisy and energetic introductory period and they do not have the confidence to see it through.

Horse owners often believe that separated horses are safer but, in actual fact, fence injuries often cause more damage than other horses.

- **Because they (the owner) are nervous of the other horses** – this can be a problem, particularly with owners who are new to horse ownership. A well - managed livery yard can go a long way to helping with this problem by having one or even two periods of each day when the herd comes in to a large central area (see the section *Implementing The Equicentral System*) and the horses are let into individual small yards for individual attention.

- **Because the horse will become too attached to the other horses** – horse owners sometimes believe that their horse will become too attached to the other horses if they are allowed to live in a herd. The opposite is actually true, because separated horses are more likely to get anxious about other horses leaving them when they are not part of a stable secure herd.

- **Because the horse will not bond with the owner** – many horse owners, and animal owners in general, believe that they will have a better 'bond' with their animal if it is deprived of the companionship of its own kind! Horses are *meant to* form stronger bonds with their own kind. It can be hard to accept this, but horses are meant to prefer the company of other horses. This does not mean that they have to dislike humans, but it is a strange horse that would choose human company over horse company!

Horse play is rough, but they should still be allowed to do it.

Enrichment for domestic horses

Enrichment means that captive/domestic animals are provided with better housing situations and stimulations that more closely replicate what they would have available to them in their natural setting. The notion of enrichment for domestic/captive animals is a relatively new concept that started in places where animals are on show - zoos. It is now more common for domestic animal owners, managers, farmers etc. to think in this way. For example, through scientific study, farmers have learned that enrichment can improve productivity of farm animals and, therefore, improvements have been and continue to be made in these areas. Of course, not all farmers needed such studies to know this, but scientific studies are very helpful if they can prove to people who believe otherwise that animals do better when they have access to better environments.

The reason this 'movement' started in zoos is *because* the animals are on public display. As society evolves, a faction of society becomes more interested in animal welfare. This has driven the changes that are now commonplace in zoos in the Western World. For example, it used to be commonplace to chain elephants to the ground for long periods, or even permanently, or to house lions separately in small cages. Depending on your age, you may be able to remember taking a trip to the zoo when you were young and seeing elephants confined in this way or a lion 'pacing' backwards and forwards in a cage. These examples are no longer accepted practice in the Western World and therefore huge changes have come about in the way zoos approach animal welfare.

The horse world has been slow to make such changes, mainly because it is so steeped in tradition. Much of what happens to horses, and in particular how they are housed, is not in the public eye. There are also many myths about what horses need and 'want'; for example we tend to anthropomorphise horses, thinking that they, like humans, want to be in a warm, safe enclosure at night. See the section **Anthropomorphising**. Perhaps this is further enhanced by the fact that our other domestic animals, cats and dogs, enjoy a warm comfy bed to sleep in, as we do. What is actually the right thing to do for our horses; providing them with simple shade/shelter but also allowing them free access to the outdoors (preferably with other horses), can sometimes seem to the uneducated as being harsh and and even cruel.

This is further complicated when some horse owners try to enrich their horse's lifestyle by keeping them outside in groups for longer periods and avoid rugging them unless absolutely necessary but are seen by the general public, and even other horse owners, who do not understand what a horse actually needs, as being cruel. Equine welfare agencies are regularly contacted by people who feel that a

94

certain horse or horses are 'not being cared-for properly', when in fact the opposite is sometimes true.

Most horses would prefer to be outside being 'horses'.

Please note: we are not totally against the use of rugging or stabling, just the over-use of them. There are some situations when we feel them to be necessary. For example, horses live much longer in the domestic situation and there comes a time, as they get older, when they struggle to keep warm without help. Also, certain breeds of horses, when kept in climates that they have not evolved to be in, can struggle to maintain body condition. This does not mean though that rugging, in particular, should be used *instead* of shade/shelter.

All horses benefit from:

- **An increase in time spent grazing** - all horses should be allowed to graze as much as possible. There is no better feed for a horse if the grass is high fibre/low sugar/starch. If the grasses are improved (e.g. high sugar/starch grasses developed for cattle), then careful management will be required to make sure that their sugar/starch intake is not too high.

- **An increase of fibre in the diet** - if you do not have enough available grazing (or the grasses are inappropriate for horses) then feed as much hay as possible. Select high fibre/low sugar/low starch hay and feed it 'ad-lib' (free choice, available 24/7). This means that the horse spends more time chewing and swallowing saliva which is what a horse is meant to do.

We are not totally against the use of rugs, however....

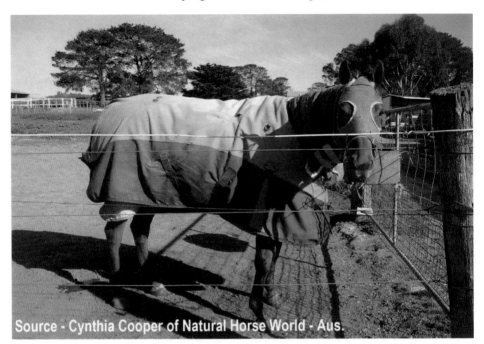
Source - Cynthia Cooper of Natural Horse World - Aus.

- **An increase in the time spent in contact with other horses at pasture** - actually *with* another horse, not just on the other side of the fence from one. Allowing horses to interact over a fence is usually far more dangerous than putting them in the same area together due to the risk of fence injuries. Horse play is rough although not usually as rough as it appears to us humans. All animals, including humans, use play as a form of development and to strengthen bonds. Even horses that appear to be low in the social structure will still choose to stay with other horses rather than be alone. In fact, two horses can seem to have a strong dislike for each other (to us humans) but if separated they may become frantic. You should therefore always aim to keep your horse/s in a herd.

- **An increase in movement** - create an environment which enables and encourages more movement. Movement is so important to a horse; millions of years of evolution have resulted in a grazing athlete that thrives on movement. When you take on horse ownership, remember that horses are meant to move, a lot! Increasing movement for your horses may mean a change of management system. See the section ***The Equicentral System*** for more information about a system that we have developed and advocate, which increases movement in horses while, at the same time, allows better land management - a win-win situation.

- **Minimisation of rugging** - rugs should only be used when necessary rather than because an owner likes to see their horse warm, clean etc. It is very easy to fall into the trap of over- rugging, simply because so many other people do it. As mentioned previously, we now have the ludicrous situation where an owner may be seen as 'cruel' if they do not rug a horse that is actually far better off without one. Remember the overuse of rugs can have implications on the weight gain/loss of horses which may lead to health concerns such as laminitis.

Horses should be allowed to graze as much as possible.

- **Minimisation of time spent in confinement** - make sure that horses are only stabled/confined when necessary. Remember, horses can give the impression that they 'like' being stabled when in fact they do not. Stables, in particular, are often no better than cages, especially those that prevent horses from even touching each other. Confining horses is often a 'necessary evil' for many horse owners because they may not have much choice if they do not own their own land. Even if they do they may not have enough land to turn horses out during wet conditions for example. In this case, aim to make sure your horse/s spends at least some time outside each day, preferably in the company of other horses. This could be a surfaced area with other horses. If you own your own horse property and already have stables established, consider changing them to a more 'horse friendly' design. This could mean making a row of stables into an open fronted 'run-in shed' etc. If you are building stables, and you are sure that you need them, consider leaving part of the stable wall open above chest height so that the horses can interact with each other.

Stables are often no better than cages, especially those that prevent horses from even touching each other.

- **An increase in the amount of time spent behaving like a real horse** - if you are aware that your horse/s live in relatively stressful conditions, aim to let them have regular 'time-out' sessions. During these times, let your horse/s go without rugs, get muddy, interact with other horses etc. Even very valuable horses can and should be allowed access to other horses. Quiet, unshod, smaller horses make great companions for large dressage horses for example (make sure they are introduced safely and properly, see the section ***Introducing horses to herd living***). Think of it as 'R and R' time. You would not like to go without your holidays, friends or general relaxation time, so don't expect your horse/s to. Keep reminding yourself that your goals are very different to the goals of your large hairy herbivore. A more relaxed 'happier' horse will ultimately be sounder, stronger, safer, healthier etc. so it will all be worthwhile in the end.

- **An increase in opportunities to make their own decisions** -this might not sound like such an important factor, although after reading this book, if you did not already see it this way, you will hopefully now appreciate the impact of decision making. Domestic horses kept in traditional management systems are not able to make many, if any, decisions in their day to day life. For some horses, literally every step they take is governed by a human, as in the case of a fully stabled horse that is only 'exercised' while being trained in an arena for example. By changing the management system, horses can be allowed to make choices, such as where they want to stand (in the shade or out in the sun etc.), which other horses they spend time with etc. This is a huge deal for a horse. See the section **The Equicentral System** which allows horses to make their own decisions as much as possible.

Let horses be horses as much as possible.

Anthropomorphising

It is a curious human characteristic to look for human behavioural traits in many things ranging from inanimate objects such as their car, to animate creatures such as their pets and other animals. Humans then use this misinformation as a reason for treating these objects or creatures in a certain way. This is not usually done with any malicious intent; quite the opposite in fact, but the problem is that while it can be fun for humans to anthropomorphise (and harmless in the case of inanimate objects such as their car); it is not helpful and can actually be harmful in the case of animals because it *disregards* an animal's real needs and *replaces* them with human needs. It is important instead to try to view horse behaviour from their perspective.

Whilst anthropomorphising can be useful in certain contexts, it is important to remember that all animal species have their own unique ethogram that has been shaped by millions of years of evolution in order to ensure species survival. An ethogram is a catalogue of behaviours which is unique to one particular animal species. These traits have been shaped in response to their natural environments, not their man-made ones. Therefore what works for us does not necessarily work for them.

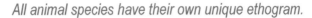

All animal species have their own unique ethogram.

The Five Freedoms

Animal welfare agencies talk about '**The Five Freedoms**' of animals. These are the five basic rights that all animals should have and are increasingly being applied to domestic and captive animals in order to provide a benchmark for their care and management. All horses have basic requirements that must be met in order for them to thrive both physically and mentally. **The Five Freedoms translated into horse parlance are:**

- *Freedom from thirst and hunger* - a horse should have ready access to fresh, clean water and sufficient amounts of the correct foodstuffs. Horse feeding practices must take into account their requirements for a very high fibre diet as that is what they have evolved to eat. Fibre should be available to a horse 24/7.

- *Freedom from discomfort* - a horse should have an appropriate environment to live in; adequate space, shade and shelter are important. Management systems must take into account normal horse behaviours. Horses are herd animals, meaning they are inherently social and require company. It is time to rethink outdated traditional management practices.

- **Freedom from pain, injury and disease** - a horse owner must know at least the basics of horse care and be able to recognise when a horse needs veterinary attention or is in need of a horse dentist, farrier or other horse health professional.

- **Freedom to express normal behaviour** - a horse owner should understand horse behaviour. This knowledge is important not only to provide suitable living conditions for any horses in their care, but also in order to train them humanely. Understanding horse behaviour is also essential for a rider or handler's safety.

- **Freedom from fear and distress** - a horse owner should not place a horse in a situation where the horse continues to suffer stress/distress; nor should a horse owner use training methods that *cause* fear, pain or distress. By using humane training methods, horses can be trained effectively and safely.

In order to make sure a horse is provided with what it *really* needs; we can turn to another simple mantra known as '**The Three F's**' - **Forage**, **Friendship**, **Freedom**. Of course there is some duplication with **The Five Freedoms**, but that just reinforces how important the basic needs of a horse really are.

The Three F's

Forage – a horse is basically a fibre processing animal whose whole psychology (behaviour) and physiology has evolved to enable it to thrive on a high fibre diet. Therefore a horse should have 'ad-lib' access to high-fibre, low energy and low protein forage.

A horse is basically a fibre processing animal whose whole psychology (behaviour) and physiology has evolved to enable it to thrive on a high fibre diet.

Friendship – horses are highly social herd animals that develop strong bonds with other horses. If we attempt to separate horses, we deny them this basic need which can cause behavioural and management issues for our horses as well as problems for our land. All horses need companionship and it is your duty as a responsible horse owner to ensure that this basic need is met. Horses need other horses for companionship; lacking other horses, they will form bonds with other animals, cattle, sheep goats etc., but there is no substitute for another horse. We as owners like to think that our horses bond with us, and they do to a certain extent, but most of that is 'cupboard love', as we provide the feed and we should never assume that we are a substitute for another horse.

Freedom - horses should be free to make choices; horses are often 'micromanaged', kept in stables, given their food in nets or buckets, brought out just to ride or train – every aspect of their lives is dictated by humans. They should have some choice in when they eat, sleep, socialise and, to a certain extent, where they want to be at different times of the day. We obviously have to make compromises due to the constraints of our boundary fences, but within these boundaries we can give our horses some choices whilst, at the same time, meeting both their needs and ours.

Horses should have some choice in when they eat, sleep, socialise and, to a certain extent, where they want to be at different times of the day.

—

The solutions to most of these issues are covered later in either this book, the other books in the series, or on our website **www.equiculture.com.au**

—

Chapter 5: Pasture/grazing management

If you have got so far in this book, you are beginning to understand, if you did not know already, why there needs to be changes to traditional horse management practices. The final chapter of this book describes a system - **The Equicentral System**, which addresses many of the issues that we have covered so far. However, in order to fully utilise this system, you also have to understand at least the basics about pasture management.

—

We hope that reading this book results in you wanting to learn even more. The second book in this series *The Equicentral System Series Book 2 - Healthy Land, Healthy Pasture, Healthy Horses* goes into these subjects in much more detail, including the 'how' as well as the 'why', but the following sections cover some of the basics that you need to understand in order to manage your land well and to implement **The Equicentral System.**

—

You need to maintain and nurture your pasture in much the same way that a farmer would, although you do not usually want the same grasses. Generally speaking, farmers require high energy (high sugar) plants for high productivity, for example, meat and milk production. Most horse owners/managers, on the other hand, require low energy (low sugar) plants because horses evolved to survive on low energy high fibre forage plus domestic horses do not tend to use up much energy as they are not usually working for a living and there are serious risks to horse health that are associated with obesity and its associated conditions. Both high energy and low energy grasses still need to be managed properly and correct management involves giving the plants time to rest and recuperate on a regular basis.

The grazing management strategies outlined in the following sections are all variations on the same theme of restricting horses to one part of the land, even though this may be a surfaced area, while the other parts get to rest, recuperate and grow more pasture.

A basic rule of thumb is that *no more than 30%* of the land should be in use at any one time. It is common on a horse property to have *all* of the land in use *all* of the time. This is called 'set-stocking' and it is *not* recommended as a good way to manage land (see the section *Set-stocking*).

The various land management strategies outlined below (with the exception of set-stocking) should be used in conjunction with one another for best results. Aim to be flexible and be prepared to change what you do to suit the current situation. For example, seasonal changes and uncharacteristic weather for the season (such as a huge downpour) will call for changes in the day-to-day routine.

A surfaced holding yard is required so that the horses can be safely confined when necessary (see the section *Constructing a holding area*). Failing that, you will need to use stables if the pasture needs a reduction in grazing pressure.

—

Grazing pressure is the stress placed on plant populations due to the grazing of animals. It includes hoof pressure as well as the actual grazing of the plant.

—

Grazing time can then be increased when pasture is available and decreased when it is not. Supplementary feed such as hay and possibly concentrates should be used to make up the shortfall (see the section *Feeding confined horses*). It is far better to confine your horses *some of the time,* if necessary, so that the time they spend in the paddocks is 'quality time' (moving and grazing grass), rather than have your horses standing around all day in bare, dusty, muddy, weedy paddocks (making them even more bare, dusty, muddy and weedy).

—

See the second book in this series *The Equicentral System Series Book 2 - Healthy Land, Healthy Pasture, Healthy Horses* for in depth information about grazing management and how you can apply this information to manage your horses and your pasture.

—

Pasture plants and grazing animals

Many pasture plants (pasture grasses in particular) have evolved to coexist with grazing animals, meaning that a symbiotic relationship exists between them and that they each rely on each other for survival. Grazing animals obviously rely on plants mainly for food. The plants rely on the grazing animals for various functions.

Grazing animals in a natural setting move across a landscape in a migratory fashion for most ruminants, and as part of a 'home-range' for most equines, biting and eating some of the plants and trampling the rest. The plants are subjected to a short, heavy period of grazing, followed by a period of rest, which stimulates them to re-grow and thicken. The animals also leave small indentations on the land with their hooves, into which some of their manure drops (along with the seeds of the plants that they have consumed in the last few days). Some of these seeds are then able to germinate and start life afresh.

In the natural situation, *various species* of animals graze and browse the plants. As different animal species favour different plant species (with some cross-overs), once all of the animals have passed over that area of grassland, the plants get chance to rest and recuperate as the animals only return periodically to the same areas.

In the natural situation, various species of animals graze and browse the plants

If they are managed properly, domestic horses and other herbivores such as cattle, sheep, goats, etc. are very beneficial to grasslands – in fact they are essential to it. Without grazing or artificial intervention such as regular mowing – which after all only attempts to copy grazing, a grassland will eventually become rank and stop growing and may ultimately even turn back to forest in some areas. It is all about *controlling* the grazing pressure so that the plants get the *beneficial effects of being grazed,* without the *negative effects of being overgrazed.* In turn, the grazing animals (horses and any other animals) get a more varied diet due to the increase in biodiversity, which is very important to all grazing animals.

What happens to pasture plants in the domestic situation is usually quite different. The practice of set-stocking is more common in a domestic situation (see the section **Set-stocking**). In reality this system is the complete opposite to how plants have evolved in the wild. As a result, instead of thriving, plants become 'stressed' and develop 'coping mechanisms' as a response to that stress. This can render grasses and other pasture plants dangerous for horses to graze (higher in sugar).

—

See the second book in this series *The Equicentral System Series Book 2 - Healthy Land, Healthy Pasture, Healthy Horses* for more information about this important relationship between grazing animals and pasture, and how you can use this information to manage your horses and your pasture.

—

Biodiversity and horses

Biodiversity is vital for a healthy environment. In a natural ecosystem, there are many types of plants, animals and insects that live alongside each other and have symbiotic relationships, meaning that they cannot survive without each other. Increasing biodiversity, therefore, is not just about taking **care** of grazing animals and the plants that they eat, but it is also about providing habitat for numerous beneficial creatures ranging from insects to insectivorous birds etc.

When biodiversity is lacking, chemicals such as pesticides and herbicides have to be relied on more and more because certain pest insects and plants become dominant as their natural predators are no longer present. The problem is that many of these chemicals, as well as causing damage to the environment, are becoming less effective as their overuse has caused resistance to build up in the plants and insects that they aim to eradicate. Due to this, there is now a lot of interest in looking at natural ways of controlling pest insects and plants.

A good, biodiverse pasture provides a wide variety of plants which contain different minerals and compounds, providing differing nutritional values and many health benefits to horses. This well-managed ecosystem also provides habitat for many other animals, some of whom predate on pest species.

A well-managed horse property can do many things to increase biodiversity. By managing the grazing of your horses, you can increase the organic mass (amount of organic matter) on your land and increase the number of plant and animal species.

Many beneficial insects live in healthy grassland. By using chemicals such as 'worming' pastes responsibly, you can reduce the damage to beneficial insects such as dung beetles. The same is true for herbicides; responsible usage means less damage to the environment. By planting trees and bushes you can provide habitat for numerous animals, such as insectivorous birds and insectivorous bats, which will in turn help to control any pest species.

A good, biodiverse pasture provides a wide variety of plants which contain different minerals and compounds, providing differing nutritional values and many health benefits to horses.

Grazing systems

Set-stocking

The incidence of 'horse-sick' pasture is usually linked to the practice of 'setstocking' the land. Set-stocking means that a given area of land is in use *all* of the time. Set-stocking is a common practice on many horse properties whereby horses are either separated into individual ('private') paddocks and these paddocks are used continuously, *or* the horses are kept as a herd but have access to all of the land continuously. In the latter example people think that they are allowing the animals to live 'more naturally', but unless there is access to very large areas of land, such as on a 'station' in the outback of Australia or a large cattle ranch in the USA, the land will degrade over time due to the relentless grazing pressure of many mouths and hooves. A further factor is that if there are only horses grazing the land, it is not benefiting from the more natural situation in which various animals would be grazing the same area.

Set-stocking the land also means that good pasture management strategies such as harrowing and mowing cannot be carried out without *increasing* the parasitic worm burden of the horses in the paddock. Larger areas also present a more difficult and time consuming job of manually clearing manure from the paddock. Set-stocking is *not* recommended as a management practice because it leads to unhealthy horses *and* unhealthy land.

—

See the second book in this series *The Equicentral System Series Book 2 - Healthy Land, Healthy Pasture, Healthy Horses* for more information about set-stocking and how you can avoid this form of land management.

—

Rotational grazing

This strategy should be used by *all* land managers so that pasture gets a period without any grazing pressure. Remember - you are aiming to copy what happens to pasture in the natural situation. Having several smaller paddocks rather than one large paddock allows the use of pasture rotation. If you already have several paddocks, but they are on the larger size, then you can subdivide/strip graze them for even better management (but aim to keep it tidy). Horses can then be moved around the property as a herd. You need to learn how to assess the pasture and decide when it is time to move the horses on to the next paddock and carry out pasture maintenance such as mowing and pasture harrowing in the one they have just finished grazing.

The incidence of 'horse-sick' pasture is usually linked to the practice of 'set-stocking' the land.

As part of your rotational grazing strategy, horses should be allowed to graze a designated paddock when the plants have reached an average height of around 15cm to 20cm (6in to 8in). Once they have grazed the paddock down to an average height of around 5cm to 8cm (2in to 3in), they should be moved to the next paddock.

When the average height of the pasture is *between* 5cm and 20cm (2in and 8in), it is generally in the elongation stage; this is when it is best able to cope with grazing pressure.

When pasture is shorter than 5cm (2in) it is in the vegetative stage and is usually unable to cope with grazing pressure *and* re-growing at the same time. Pasture plants need a certain amount of leaf content to make use of sunlight and moisture from rain and dew. If they are continuously grazed when too short they will take longer to recover if and when conditions improve, they may also become totally exhausted and die out.

Short, stressed grass plants have higher sugar levels per mouthful, as they store sugar waiting for the right conditions to re-grow.

In this vegetative state the grass contains relatively high concentrations of NSC (non structural carbohydrates, in the form of sugars and starches). **Research has shown that excessive NSC levels are strongly linked with laminitis**, therefore, very short grass can actually be dangerous for fat and laminitic prone horses to graze.

When the pasture plants reach the reproductive stage (generally longer than 20cm - 8in) the seed heads form and they stop growing. At this stage the plants are relatively high in sugar but eventually, when many of the seeds have dropped, the plants are relatively high in fibre.

Once they have grazed the paddock down to an average height of around 5cm to 8cm (2in to 3in), they should be moved to the next paddock.

—

See the second book in this series ***The Equicentral System Series Book 2 - Healthy Land, Healthy Pasture, Healthy Horses*** for in depth information about managing grasses, managing a horse's weight and pasture maintenance/management in general.

—

Limited grazing

The term 'limited grazing' means that you allow the horses to graze a designated paddock for only *part of the time* (in conjunction with rotational grazing). To do so, you might keep the horses confined either overnight or through the day. This strategy is carried out on a horse property for two main reasons: 1) to reduce grazing pressure so that land does not become overgrazed and 2) to reduce the pasture intake of horses, although this does not always work as intended – (see below). In some areas, horse owners also confine horses overnight for their safety due to the presence of wild/feral animals.

Removing horses for a period each day vastly reduces the amount of time they spend sleeping or loafing on the pasture, and thereby reduces land degradation. When horses are removed from pasture for a period of time and are then returned, they tend to get straight down to grazing rather than standing around. Another alternative is to let the horses graze for two shorter periods per day, rather than one long one, but this means that the horses have to be led in and out two times a day rather than one.

The Equicentral System described in this book allows the horses to come and go as they wish. This adds important decision making opportunities as they *voluntarily* remove their grazing pressure. If necessary, the horses can *also* be confined for part of each day (limited grazing) for the reasons outlined above.

Keep in mind though that a horse will attempt to concentrate their grazing bouts into the period in which they are turned out. So, restricting a horse by locking them up and then turning them out does *not* really reduce their intake unless the turnout time is very short. For example, if you confine a horse for eight hours and turn them out for 16 hours, the horse will concentrate their grazing bouts into this 16 hour period. Therefore doing this simply results in them gorging themselves when turned out. Never starve confined horses by restricting hay – see the section *Feeding confined horses*.

Limited grazing is an excellent strategy for reducing land degradation *and* for making your available pasture last as long as possible. It may not be as effective at controlling your horse's intake, although if necessary, by reducing the turn out period significantly, you can reduce intake to some extent; however horses should always have access to low sugar, high fibre hay.

Removing horses for a period each day vastly reduces the amount of time they spend sleeping or loafing on the pasture, and thereby reduces land degradation.

See the second book in this series *The Equicentral System Series Book 2 - Healthy Land, Healthy Pasture, Healthy Horses* for more information about limited grazing including some of the things that you need to be aware of, how you can implement it etc.

Strip grazing

This strategy involves using portable electric fencing to *reduce* the area of the paddock currently available to the horses. It is commonly used with cows in the dairy industry to make the available pasture last *as long* as possible, but many horse owners also use this grazing management strategy. Horses are very selective grazers and, if they have access to a large area for too long, they will overgraze some areas and under graze others. Eventually, the land will develop that characteristic 'horse-sick' appearance (see the section **The 'dunging behaviour' of domestic horses**). By having their access restricted to a smaller area, the horses will graze more evenly on the available pasture and, at the same time, the fenced-off area is allowed to be in the rest and recuperation phase for longer, resulting in more pasture growth. Strip grazing is actually rotational grazing to an even greater degree.

Horse owners are sometimes concerned that reducing the paddock size will reduce the horse's movement but in fact, as strip grazing encourages more biodiversity by allowing different plants to survive and thrive, this encourages movement; horses move more on biodiverse pasture than they do on a 'mono culture' of just one type of pasture plant.

Take care that you do not allow the area that is currently being grazed to be overgrazed. You still need to adhere to the same plant lengths as for rotational grazing (see the section **Rotational grazing**).

—

The Equicentral System described later in this book lends itself well to strip grazing, because water is not an issue as it is always back in the surfaced holding yard where the horses can always get to it. If the position of the temporary fence results in a narrow section near a gateway, as is often the case when 'fanning' the fence out from a corner, this is also not a problem because the horses will not be trapped in this relatively narrow area as they can instead continue on to the surfaced holding yard (see the section **The Equicentral System**).

—

Further manipulation of the grazing area can be achieved by 'block grazing' which is the addition of a second temporary fence across the area that has already been grazed in order to prevent the animals from grazing back over it. Temporary laneways are yet another way that you can better utilise the land that you have – see the section *Temporary laneways*).

Subdividing larger paddocks by using strip grazing and its variations has many benefits over permanently fencing more and smaller paddocks. It saves the considerable expense of erecting and maintaining extra, permanent fencing and also allows much more flexibility in terms of pasture maintenance - for example, a vehicle such as a tractor can turn more easily in a larger area - and the larger area can be used for haymaking when necessary.

—

See the second book in this series *The Equicentral System Series Book 2 - Healthy Land, Healthy Pasture, Healthy Horses* for more information about strip grazing/block grazing, including some of the things that you need to be aware of, how you can implement them etc.

—

Cross-grazing

'Cross-grazing' is a term used to describe the practice of using more than one species of grazing animal to graze a pasture. Cross-grazing occurs naturally in the 'wild' of course, and there are various advantages to implementing it in the domestic situation . **Using other species of grazing animal to help with grazing management has two main advantages:**

'Cross-grazing' is a term used to describe the practice of using more than one species of grazing animal to graze a pasture.

- Different animal species tend to complement each other in their grazing behaviours by eating different plants and different parts of the same plants. Sheep and goats, in particular, will eat woodier plants that are often left behind by horses, and can also safely eat some weeds that can be harmful to horses.

Because these other animals eat the parts of the pasture that the horses tend to ignore, including the 'roughs', having more animals does not always mean more total grazing pressure as it would if you simply added more horses. Crossgrazing results in more 'even grazing' of a pasture e.g. reduces 'roughs' and 'lawns'. Furthermore, cloven hoofed sheep and cattle reduce solid compression.

- As mentioned before different animal species will eat around the dung of other species, but not that of their own.

The most common animals used for cross-grazing are cows and sheep however you can also use other animals such as goats, llamas and alpacas. Donkeys do not count as they are the same species as horses – equines. Wildlife can also have cross-grazing benefits – it all depends on your locality as to which wild animals may also graze your land.

—

See the second book in this series *The Equicentral System Series Book 2 - Healthy Land, Healthy Pasture, Healthy Horses* for more information about cross-grazing including some of the things that you need to be aware of, how you can implement it etc.

—

Basic pasture maintenance

This involves spreading manure (if you are not picking it up) and mowing any long grass that has not been eaten by the horses. Both of these procedures should be done once the horses have been rotated on to the next paddock.

If you are carrying out cross-grazing, however, you may not need to mow because the land will have been grazed more evenly by the different animal species.

Mowing a paddock after the horses have been moved on means that all the plants are cut-back to the same length – and will regrow reasonably evenly. If it is not carried out, the plants remain at different heights. Remember, pasture plants do not re-grow until they are grazed or cut back; this is one of the reasons that 'horse-sick' paddocks have that bedraggled appearance, because some areas of the paddock (the 'roughs') are never grazed or mown.

Mowing encourages the grass to thicken and improves coverage. It also means that organic matter (from the cut plants) ends up on the ground and decomposes, improving the soil.

Mowing also helps to control upright weeds (but not weeds that grow along the ground, known as prostrate weeds) because many weeds do not thrive when cut back. Cutting a *grass* plant mimics the grazing of an animal and stimulates the plant to start growing again. Therefore, a timely mowing favours grass plants and gives them a competitive advantage over many weeds. It is better to cut weeds before they go to seed so that you do not spread seeds around the paddock.

Harrowing (picture a) involves dragging an implement around the paddock to break up and spread the manure piles. Mowing a paddock (picture b) after the horses have been moved on means that all the plants are cut-back to the same length.

Spreading manure around a paddock, rather than allowing it to stay in the areas that horses deposit it, results in more uniform grazing behaviour in the future. The whole paddock benefits from the nutrients and organic matter in the manure and spreading manure also helps to kill some of the parasitic 'worms' in the paddock.

The eggs and larvae of parasitic 'worms' need lots of moisture to survive and, once a ball of manure is broken up, many of them are killed by sunshine or frost. Harrowing is best done before a period of sunshine in order to help destroy parasite eggs and larvae?

Harrowing is a manure management strategy which has the added benefit of improving pasture. Harrowing involves dragging an implement around the paddock to break up and spread the manure piles. The aim is to ensure that each and every pile of manure is broken up and scattered. If your land is not level, you need harrows that are flexible to get into all the contours of your land. Commercial harrows usually have spikes that also scratch the surface as they spread manure; this means they can pull out old, dead plants and create grooves for new seeds to get established, but it is the manure spreading function that is the most important.

—

See the second book in this series *The Equicentral System Series Book 2 - Healthy Land, Healthy Pasture, Healthy Horses* for more information about pasture maintenance strategies such as mowing and harrowing including some of the things that you need to be aware of, how you can implement them etc.

—

Putting it all together

The use of various grazing management strategies offers great results for your land. If this all seems a little complicated, try to remember that rotational grazing is the main management strategy you should use. Pasture must have periods where it is allowed to rest and recuperate and therefore all land managers need to use this strategy so that paddocks get periods without any grazing pressure at all. Remember - the aim is to have healthy, vigorous plants, not stressed, worn out plants. The other grazing management strategies such as limited grazing, strip grazing and cross-grazing are used in conjunction with rotational grazing to 'fine tune' grazing pressure.

The next chapter is about The Equicentral System, a total management system that gives you even more control over grazing pressure and has big benefits for you, your horses and the environment.

Chapter 6: The Equicentral System

The Equicentral System is a *total* horse and land management system that we have developed and have been teaching to horse owners around the world for many years now. It uses the natural and domestic behaviour of horses, combined with good land management practices, to create a healthy and sustainable environment for your horses, the land that they live on *and* the wider environment.

There are many examples in various countries including Australia, New Zealand, the UK, the USA and even Panama! This this list just keeps growing as people realise the huge benefits of using **The Equicentral System** in order to manage their horses *and* their land in a sustainable way.

How The Equicentral System works

The Equicentral System utilises the natural grazing and domestic paddock behaviour of horses in order to benefit the land that they live on *and* the wider environment. In turn this benefits the horses and it also benefits you (and your family) because it saves you money and time/labour.

- The main facilities – water, shade/shelter, hay and any supplementary feed are positioned in a surfaced holding yard so that the horses *can always* get back to them from the pasture they are currently grazing.

- The watering points are *only situated in the surfaced holding yard*, instead of there being one in each paddock. If you already have water troughs' situated in paddocks these can be turned off when horses are using the paddock, and turned back on again if and when other animals, such as cows or sheep, are grazing there.

- Individual water troughs/drinkers (or buckets) of course are also needed in any individual yards/stables.

- If possible all of the paddocks *are linked* to this surfaced holding yard area, although only one paddock is in use at any time.

- The gate to the paddock that is currently in use *is always* open, so that the horses *can always* get themselves back to the water/shade/shelter etc. *In short, the horses are never shut out of the surfaced holding yard*.

- Occasionally they may be fastened in the surfaced holding yard (with hay), but this is usually for the purpose of preventing damage to the land and increasing healthy pasture production.

- Apart from trees or bushes that are situated in/around paddocks, **the only shade/shelter is in the surfaced holding yard**. This shade/shelter is very important. It should be large enough for the whole herd to benefit from it at the same time.

The Equicentral System: *all of the paddocks lead back to the surfaced holding yard. There is shade/shelter and water in this central area. Hay can also be fed here.*

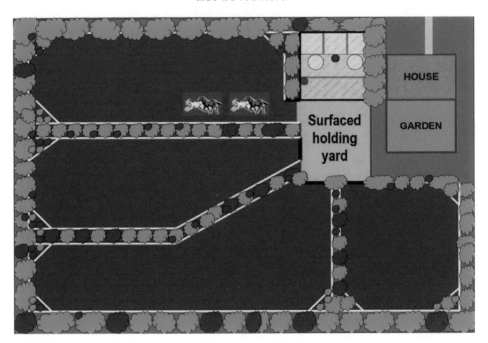

Additional information

- The surfaced holding yard area *can* also be a riding/training surface if that is what you wish. You may prefer to keep it separate or indeed you may not need a riding/training surface - but if you do then this means that the expense of creating this surfaced area has double benefits. This could mean that you are able to afford and justify this surfaced area sooner because you are going to get more use out of it. Also remember, the smaller the property, the more the facilities need to be dual purpose whenever possible so that you have as much land in use as pasture as possible.

- Careful consideration of the surface is required, especially if it is to be a riding/training surface as well. Remember - bare dirt is not an option. Wet mud is dangerously slippery and can harbour viruses and bacteria which can affect

118

the horses legs. Mud will become and dusty when dry, meaning that the horses will be breathing in potential contaminants *and* you will be losing top soil.

The surfaced holding yard area can also be a riding/training surface if that is what you wish. If you do then this means that the expense of creating this surfaced area has double benefits.

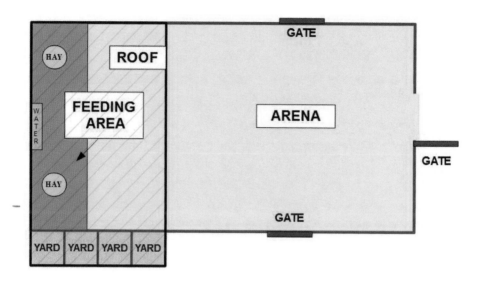

—

See the third book in this series for more information about using a surfaced holding yard as a riding surface as well, *The Equicentral System Series Book 3 – Horse Property Planning and Development.*

—

- It is useful if there are also some individual holding yards (or stables if you already have them) – preferably linked to the surfaced holding yard for ease of use. You can then separate horses into them for any individual attention that they may require (such as grooming, supplementary feeding etc.) or for tacking up etc. You can also put the surplus horses in them if you are riding/training one of the herd members on the larger surfaced holding yard.

- This system is *not* about food restriction – quite the opposite. It is about transitioning horses to an ad-lib feeding regime of low energy pasture plants and hay (see the section *Changing your horse/s to 'ad-lib' feeding*).so that they no longer gorge and put weight on because of it.

- Your pasture may need to be transitioned to lower energy plants. This does not always mean reseeding.

119

—

This is too large a subject to cover here and is covered in the second book in this series *The Equicentral System Series Book 2 - Healthy Land, Healthy Pasture, Healthy Horses.*

—

- Hay can be fed in the larger surfaced holding yard if the horses get on well enough; generally horses will share hay. Otherwise, it can be fed in the individual holding yards/stables, but keep in mind that there should *always* be some form of feed available to the horses.

- It can be a good idea to create a feeding area in the larger surfaced holding yard using large rubber mats or similar.

It is useful if there are also some individual holding yards (or stables if you already have them) – preferably linked to the surfaced holding yard for ease of use. These individual yards can be made from swing away partitions if you only require them periodically (picture left) or can be permanently in place (picture right).

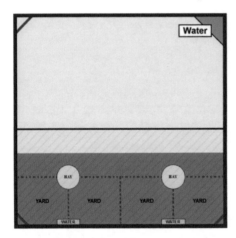 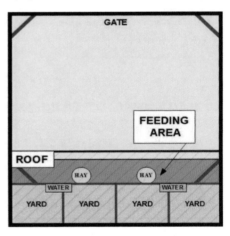

- **The Equicentral System** works best on a property where the horses live together as one herd, otherwise you will need to replicate it for each group of horses that you have. However, many of our clients however have done just that in the case of larger properties with various classes of horses (for example studs, livery yards etc.).

- **The Equicentral System** assumes that you already have good grazing management in place (rotational grazing) or that you plan to implement it. Remember, rotational grazing involves moving the animals around the land as a herd, one paddock at a time, rather than allowing them access to the whole property at once (set-stocking).

The Equicentral System in practice

This is an example of how **The Equicentral System** works in practice. In this example, the horses are being kept in the surfaced holding yard at night (or in individual holding yards/stables) and out at pasture through the day, but remember - if there is enough pasture, then the horses do not need to be confined overnight unless you have other reasons for doing so.

- In the morning you open the surfaced holding yard/riding arena gate and the horses **walk themselves** to the paddock that is currently in use for a grazing bout (which lasts between 1.5 to 3 hours), the gate to this paddock should already be open (the other paddocks should have closed gates as they are being rested).

- At all times the horses are free to return to the surfaced holding yard for a drink, but they usually won't bother until they have finished their grazing bout.

- After drinking, the shade and inviting surface in the surfaced holding yard encourages the horses to rest (loaf) in this area before returning to the paddock for another grazing bout later in the day.

After a grazing bout, the horses return to the surfaced holding yard for a drink.

- Leaving hay in the surfaced holding yard can encourage even more time being spent (voluntarily) in the surfaced holding yard and less time spent in the paddock.

- At the end of the day, the horses return from the paddock to the surfaced holding yard to await you and any supplementary feed that they may be receiving.

- You simply close the gate preventing them from returning to the paddock for the night, or, if conditions allow it, the horses can come and go through the night as well as through the day.

After drinking, the shade and inviting surface in the surfaced holding yard encourages the horses to rest (loaf) in this area before returning to the paddock for another grazing bout later in the day.

The Equicentral System benefits

The Equicentral System utilises the natural and domestic behaviour of horses to better manage the land that they live on. **This system of management has many, many benefits including:**

Horse health/welfare benefits:

- It encourages horses to move more and movement is good; a grazing horse is a moving horse. A recent (Australian) study showed that horses in a 0.8 Ha. paddock walked approximately 4.5km per day, even when water was situated in the paddock; additional movement to the water in the surfaced holding yard, therefore, further increases this figure. More movement also means better hoof quality as the hooves rely on movement to function properly. Remember a healthy, biodiverse pasture encourages more movement.

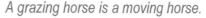

A grazing horse is a moving horse.

- It *maximises* time spent grazing for horses and aims to avoid food restriction. By confining horses initially and when the weather is very dry or very wet (or in order to transition horses that have been on restricted diets in the past), so that the pasture begins to improve, becomes more biodiverse etc. they will be able to graze more in the future because healthy pasture can withstand more grazing.

- Horses are not being forced to stand in mud, especially around gateways when weather conditions are wet. Horses are not good at coping with continuous wet conditions – hence the ease with which they develop skin conditions such as greasy heel/mud fever. Remember - in the naturally-living situation, they will *take themselves* to higher, dryer ground to loaf, even if the areas that they graze are wet. When horses are fastened in wet paddocks, they do not have this choice.

The horses will be able to graze more in the future because healthy pasture can withstand more grazing.

- Eliminating mud also means eliminating dust because they derive from the same thing (bare soil) at either end of a spectrum. Apart from the obvious benefits to not losing your top soil, this means that horses (and humans) do not have to cope with living in a dusty environment.

- Horses move around a paddock in a natural fashion, choosing what to eat. As rotational grazing increases the diversity of plants in a pasture, the horses benefit from access to a larger variety of plants. This means that the horses eat a more natural, varied diet. In addition, healthier plants are safer to graze than stressed, overgrazed plants (more fibre and less sugar per mouthful).

—

See the second book in this series *The Equicentral System Series Book 2 - Healthy Land, Healthy Pasture, Healthy Horses* for much more information on this subject.

—

- The stress of not being able to get to food at will, along with all of its associated problems, is removed. Horses with different dietary requirements can be catered for with the addition of supplementary daily feed (in a separate but preferably adjoining area).

- The surfaced holding yard is seen by the horses as a good place to be and therefore, if and when it is necessary to fasten them in there, (bad weather, for the vet etc.) they are not stressed.

- The horses now have choice; they can choose as a herd whether to graze, walk to the 'water hole', snooze in the shade etc. Instead of us deciding when a grazing bout will start/finish, the horses can decide for themselves. These are all behaviours that naturally-living horses take for granted, but domestic horses are usually 'micro managed' in such a way that a human decides where they will be at any point in the day. This might not seem like a big deal but it really is.

The Equicentral System provides a 'home-range' whereby the horses can access the available resources in a more natural fashion.

Time saving benefits:

- You do not have to lead horses in and out to the pasture. The horses are waiting for you close to the house, or at least in an area where you need them to be, much of the time. If they are currently grazing, you simply call them; horses soon learn to come to a call for a reward. This means that when you return from work and the weather is bad, you do not need to trail out in the wind and the rain to bring them in, they will be waiting for you in the surfaced holding yard.

- You do not have to spend time carting feed around the property (or keep a vehicle especially for the job) because the horses *bring themselves* to the surfaced holding yard for feed. The horses *move themselves* around the property, *taking themselves* out to the paddock that they are currently grazing, and bringing *themselves* back for water and feed.

- The single water trough in the surfaced holding yard is all that you have to check each morning and night, saving you having to go out to a paddock and check the water.

- It is far quicker to pick up manure from the surfaced holding yard than from pasture if you collect your manure.

- Any time you save can be spent on other horse pursuits such as exercising them!

You do not have to spend time carting feed around the property.

Cost saving benefits:

- Money spent on the surfaced holding yard is money well spent, as this area is used *every day of the year* for *at least twelve hours* a day, even if you are not also using this surface for riding/training.

- Money spent on vet bills for treating skin and hoof conditions is reduced or totally eliminated.

- The expense of installing and/or maintaining a water trough in each paddock is spared.

- The expense of installing individual shade/shelters in each paddock is spared. Instead, one large shade/shelter is erected at the side of or over the surfaced holding yard, which means you may end up with a partially covered all weather riding/training surface if you are multi-tasking this area!

- This large shade/shelter will be in use *every day* of the year, unlike shade/shelters that are situated in paddocks and are only in use when the paddock is in use. Remember - if you are rotating your paddocks (as part of a rotational grazing management system), then this means that each paddock will be empty, and any shade/shelters situated in them will be unused, for a large part of each year.

- Annual maintenance including time and expense, of numerous shelters (especially if they are made of wood) is avoided adding to the cost effectiveness of **The Equicentral System**.

- Many horse properties already have the facilities required to implement **The Equicentral System**. Often the required infrastructure either already exists on a horse property, or the property needs minimal changes.

- Laneways (and their associated costs) can be kept to a minimum. In areas that *do* require laneways, any money spent on surfacing them is well utilised as the laneways will be used by the horses several times a day.

This large shade/shelter will be in use every day of the year, unlike shade/shelters that are situated in paddocks and are only in use when the paddock is in use.

- Better land management means more pasture to use for grazing (and safer healthier pasture) and more opportunities for conserving pasture (as 'standing hay' for example) or making hay. This all leads to much less money being spent on bought-in feed.

- You do not need to buy and maintain a vehicle for 'feeding out'. The horses come to where the feed is stored rather than you having to trail around the paddocks 'feeding out'.

- Setting up **The Equicentral System** will not devalue your land. It will actually increase the value of it through good land management. Likewise, if you sell the property, the next owner can choose to set up a more traditional management system by putting water and shade/shelter in every paddock if they wish.

Safety benefits:

- Horses move themselves around the property, therefore there is less unnecessary contact between humans and horses. This is an important point if you have (usually less experienced) family or friends taking care of your horses when you are away. **The Equicentral System** allows them to see to your horses without them having to catch and lead them around the property.

- It reduces or eliminates the incidence of horses and people being together in a paddock gateway. When horses are led out to a paddock, they can be excited because they are about to be freed; and when they are waiting at a gate to come back in for supplementary feed, they are keen get through the gateway in the other direction for their feed. Horses can crowd each other and human handlers can become trapped. These situations are very high risk on a horse property.

- Depending on its position, the surfaced holding yard can be a firebreak (for your home) and a relatively safe refuge in times of fire/storm/flood for your horses. The layout of the property may result in the horses being pushed (by rising water) back towards the surfaced holding yard in a flood. Assuming the surfaced holding yard is built on higher ground, this can save lives! By training the horses to always come back on a call, you can get them into the surfaced holding yard quickly in any emergency situation. This makes it far easier for you, your neighbours, or the emergency services to evacuate your horses if necessary in emergency situations.

Land/environmental management benefits:

- **The Equicentral System** is a *sustainable* system that acknowledges that a horse is *part of* an ecosystem, not separate to it.

- **The Equicentral System** complements a rotational grazing land management system and allows for the fine tuning of it. Remember - rotational grazing encourages healthy pasture growth and aids biodiversity by moving the animals to the next grazing area before they overgraze some of the less persistent plant varieties.

- With good land management, the productivity of biodiverse, safer pasture should *increase* rather than decrease over time, leading to fewer periods when it is necessary to fasten horses in the surfaced holding yard over time. Remember - biodiversity is good for horses *and* good for the environment.

- It *vastly* reduces land degradation that would be caused by unnecessary grazing pressure. The horses *voluntarily* reduce their time spent on the pasture.

They will tend to spend the same amount of time grazing (as they would if they were fastened in a paddock for 24 hours), but will tend to carry out any other behaviours in the surfaced holding yard.

They will tend to carry out any other behaviours in the surfaced holding yard.

- They prefer the surfaced holding yard not least because, if it is situated near the house, or at least in an area that they can see you coming towards them, no self-respecting horse will miss an opportunity to keep watch for the possibility of supplementary feed! The water and shade in the surfaced holding yard also encourages the horses to loaf in this area. If the horses are allowed to come and go night and day they will reduce the grazing pressure (grazing pressure being a combination of actually eating but also standing around on the land) by approximately 50%. If you fasten them in the surfaced holding yard (with hay) overnight, you will further reduce the grazing pressure by about another 50% (making a total of about 75%). This reduction in grazing pressure will make a *huge* difference to the land.

- The corresponding compacted soil/muddy areas that surround water troughs and paddock shelters, as well as the tracks that develop in a paddock are avoided. Bare/muddy/dusty gateways are also a thing of the past as horses are *never* fastened in a paddock waiting to come in. Don't forget that the idea is to reduce any unnecessary pressure on your valuable pasture and increase movement. Remember - the reason horses stand in gateways is because that is usually the nearest point to supplementary food; they are either fed in that area or their owner leads them from there to a surfaced holding yard or stable to feed them. If the gate is closed, they stand there; if the gate is open, they bring themselves into the surfaced area, which becomes their favourite loafing area.

—

Managing your land in this way results in less or no soil loss, in fact if you manage your land well you should be able to increase soil production – see the second book in this series *The Equicentral System Series Book 2 - Healthy Land, Healthy Pasture, Healthy Horses*.

—

- It reduces the area of land used for laneways and therefore the land degradation caused by them – by minimising laneways as much as possible. This is done by creating a layout whereby the paddocks lead directly to the surfaced holding area or by creating temporary laneways. If paddocks are already fenced and laneways are in place then this system utilises them efficiently and safely e.g. the horses are not fastened in narrow areas, they can spread out when they reach the paddock at one end or the surfaced holding yard at the other.

- It increases water quality – by minimising or eliminating soil and nutrient runoff. Rotational grazing maintains better plant cover – the absolute best way to keep soil and nutrients on the land and out of the waterways.

- Strip grazing is usually easier to set up because the water point is back in the surfaced holding yard, meaning that the fence only has to funnel the horses back to the gate, without having to take the water trough position into consideration.

- Hay is fed in the surfaced holding yard area rather than the paddocks allowing for better weed control.

Public perception benefits:

- **The Equicentral System** helps to create a positive image of horsekeeping.

- **The Equicentral System** is most likely to be regarded as a good way to manage land by landowners, the general public and the local authorities. There is a general expectation that land should be well managed - e.g. less mud/dust and fewer weeds rather than more mud/dust and weeds.

- **The Equicentral System** fulfils this expectation, creating a positive image of horse ownership rather than a negative one. This is an important point, remember - in some areas legislation is being pushed forward to reduce horse-keeping activities due to the negative image caused by the often poor land management practices on many horse properties.

- In particular, as horses are often kept on land that is leased rather than land that is owned by the horse owner, the landowner usually, and quite rightly, expects to see good land management taking place. Of course horse owners that own their own land should, and usually do, want the same.

There is a general expectation that land should be well managed - e.g. less mud/dust and fewer weeds.

Manure and parasitic worm management benefits:

- The manure, along with the horses, comes to you. More manure is dropped in the surfaced holding yard and much less in the paddocks (as much as 75% less if you fasten the horses in the surfaced holding yard/s at night with hay). This allows for much better manure management.

- If you usually collect manure that is dropped on pasture then it is physically easier to pick up manure from the surfaced holding yard/s.

- This collected manure can then be composted (which also reduces parasites on your property, as thorough composting can kill parasitic worm eggs and larvae).

- Composted manure is much better 'product' than 'fresh' manure.

- Less manure on the pasture is less importunity for parasitic worm larvae to attach to pasture plants.

- Better manure management also means less reliance on worming chemicals.

- The extra pasture created by managing the land better increases the possibility of being able to 'cross-graze' (graze other species of animals on the land). This further reduces parasitic worms on the land in the most natural way possible, because parasitic worms are what is termed 'host specific', meaning that they can only survive when picked up by the host animal that they evolved alongside.

- Rotational grazing also aids in parasitic worm management by increasing the time that a given area of pasture is resting, which means that *some* of the parasitic worm larvae (on the pasture) dry out and die as they wait - in vain! - for a horse to eat the plant that they are attached to.

—

See the second book in this series **The Equicentral System Series Book 2 - Healthy Land, Healthy Pasture, Healthy Horses** for detailed information about manure management including many novel ideas such as how chickens can be used to help you to manage horse manure.

—

Manure dropped on the surfaced yard rather than pasture is also far preferable in terms of parasitic worm management (no plants to attach to for any larvae that hatch out).

Implementing The Equicentral System

This section describes some of the practicalities of implementing **The Equicentral System**. In some sections you will be referred on to one of the other books in the series because there is too much information to be covered here.

On your own land

Obviously, this is what most people aspire to; having their own land. If you are in this fortunate position, then you are free to set up **The Equicentral System** and reap the benefits.

If you are fortunate enough to own your own land then you are free to set up **The Equicentral System** *and reap the benefits.*

On small areas of land

The Equicentral System is the ideal way to manage horses when there is only a small area of land available for grazing. In fact, it is the only way that will ensure that the horses have grazing available to them and at the same time, land degradation is not created. Of course it will mean that the horses are not able to graze as much as they or you would like, but at least the grazing they do have will be 'quality' grazing rather than standing around on bare, dusty/muddy, weedy land. So don't ever think that your situation would not support **The Equicentral System**, because it will.

At least the grazing they do have will be 'quality' grazing.

Source - Alayne Blickle of Horses for Clean Water - USA.

A common scenario, especially when people lease land, is that they have just one paddock (picture A). Even in this situation it is not difficult to set up **The Equicentral System**. You can still make huge changes to your management of the land and horses by creating a fenced hard standing area by the gate (surfaced holding yard) preferable with a shade/shelter. The 'paddocks' can fan out from this area (picture B). The facilities/fencing can be made temporary/relocatable materials including sectional holding yard fences and rubber paving mesh for the surfaced holding yard and electric fencing for the internal fences.

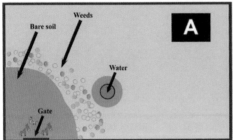
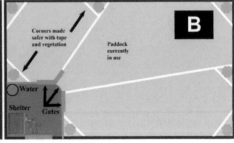

On large areas of land

The Equicentral System works well on a large 'mixed use' property as well as on a large horse property such as a stud. Other species of grazing animals respond well to having a centralised area for resources so it is possible to set up multiple central holding areas on large properties that have different types of grazing animals. Likewise, a large horse stud that has various age groups of horses can also have multiple central points.

*In this example (on a 100 ac/40 he property) there is an **Equicentral System** set up for the horses, positioned near the house as the owners will be handling the horses much more regularly than they will the cattle. The central area for the cattle is at the bottom of the hill, well away from the house. Occasionally the owners can bring the cattle up the hill (via the driveway or through various paddocks) so that the horse paddocks can benefit from cross grazing.*

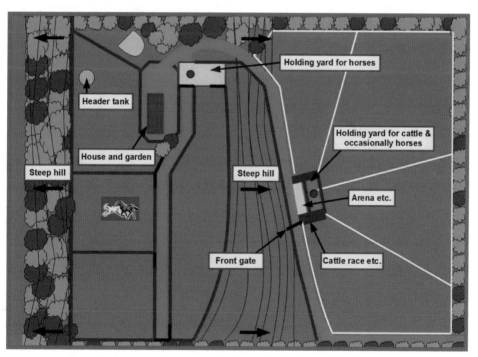

*Two **Equicentral Systems** in place. When the youngstock need to be brought up to the main yard near the house, the mares and foals are fastened in one of the paddocks.*

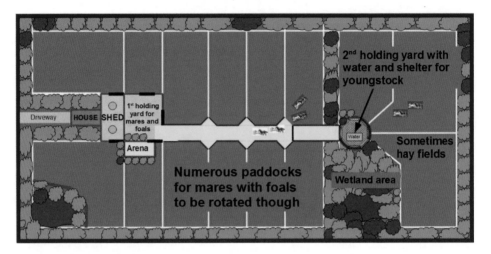

In different climates

The Equicentral System works equally well in any climate, whether it be temperate/wet/tropical/dry/arctic etc. This is because you are providing a 'home range' for the horses and allowing them (most of the time) to make the decisions about when to graze and when to shade/shelter. So, when insects are particularly problematic, they can *take themselves* to the shade to escape them and when they need fibre, they can decide for themselves when to go out to graze or to stay in the shade/shelter and eat hay (if you leave 'ad-lib' hay in the shelter). When it is very cold and wet, they can decide to shelter mainly at night and graze mainly by day. You only need to step in and 'micro manage' them when they are about to put too much pressure on the land that would lead to less pasture in the future.

Yes it is good to understand different land class types and understand what sort of soil you have, but initially it is more important that you understand that land and climates tend to range from too wet to too dry.

Either way, as long as you have an area to allow the horses to remove the pressure voluntarily, as well as involuntarily when you decide that the land needs a hand; you will see a reduction in, and eventually an elimination of dust and mud and its associated problems.

Using existing facilities

If your land already has facilities in place, **The Equicentral System** can usually be implemented without making any major structural changes to your property. **For example:**

- Hard standing that is already in place around any farm buildings/stables etc. should be able to be utilised as a surfaced holding yard. So, if you already have a 'stable yard' that has hard-standing with the paddocks leading out from this area, then you already have a great set up.

- In many cases it is just a matter of leaving the gate to the paddock that is currently in-use open so that the horses can get back to this area, rather than fastening them on the other side of the gate.

- Old farm buildings can usually be used to great effect, as long as they are safe and have a high enough roof for horses. Such buildings often already have hard standing in and around them.

An old farm building such as this would be great for converting to a 'run-in shed' for horses.

- By implementing rotational grazing and always having the gate open to the paddock they are currently using, the horses will bring themselves back to the yard and stand on the surfaced area, rather than stand in the gateway and create mud.

- You can turn off the water in the paddocks (or stop carrying water out to the paddocks!), and set up a water trough on the hard-standing area.

- You may want to create extra shade/shelter for the horses by using the existing buildings to fasten 'shade sails' from, or extend the roof area with a more solid style of roof.

- If you have a block of stables you may decide to open the fronts of some or all of the individual stables boxes to create a 'run-in shed'. Keep in mind that, for various reasons such as tacking up, health care/vet work/trimming/shoeing, supplementary feeding etc., it is still useful to have some individual holding areas.

- Surplus stables can be used for storing hay etc.

By implementing rotational grazing and always having the gate open to the paddock they are currently using, the horses will bring themselves back to the stable yard and stand on the surfaced area, rather than stand in the gateway and create mud.

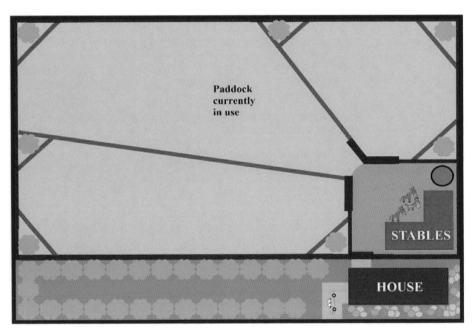

You may want to create extra shade/shelter for the horses by using the existing buildings to fasten 'shade sails' from, or extend the roof area with a more solid style of roof.

Source - Alayne Blickle of Horses for Clean Water - USA.

On land that you lease

A landowner should be happy for you to implement a system of management that is going improve their land value. For example, horse owners often lease land from farmers and most farmers understand the value of a rotational grazing system.

If you need more land and you are already demonstrating good land management techniques, then you are more likely to be given the opportunity to lease/use that additional land than someone who is not doing so. For example, it is not uncommon for neighbours that have land they are not using to offer it to someone with grazing animals. However, they are unlikely to do this if they see that the land you are currently using is badly managed.

In this situation you may want to use facilities/materials that can be removed and taken with you if you ever move on. There are various options for temporary/relocatable shade/shelters (that have the added advantage of not usually requiring planning permission), fences (including sectional holding yard fences) and even surfaces (such as rubber paving mesh).

—

See the third book in this series *The Equicentral System Series Book 3 – Horse Property Planning and Development* for lots of ideas and solutions.

—

On a livery yard (boarding/agistment facility)

It is perfectly possible to have this system in operation on a horse livery yard. If the horses already live in herds, then the issues are just the same as for setting this system up on a private-use property. If they do not, then first you have to establish the logistics of how you will integrate the horses into herds. There are several options. You may decide to have a mare group and a gelding group (or several depending on the numbers). You may have a variety of groups, for example, you may decide to let owners group their horses so that they are able to share horse-keeping duties with friends.

Hopefully, the property does not currently have a single horse shade/shelter in every paddock as these will be too small for grouped horses.

Small paddocks that previously housed one horse each can now be rotationally grazed. A central holding yard area will need to be constructed for each herd.

If you wish to implement this system and you would prefer that the owners do not enter a paddock containing a large herd of horses, then you can create a routine whereby the horses come into individual areas once or even twice a day (preferably these areas should lead off from the large surfaced holding yard). This can be very useful in cases of horses receiving different levels of supplementary feed etc.

With single horses in 'private paddocks'

Please note: we are not advocating keeping horses separate to each other, but some owners will *never* put their horse with another horse and very occasionally there are good reasons for separating horses.

Separated horses can still benefit from better pasture management and a better shade/shelter arrangement that allows some socialisation, if it is not already in place.

Horses in 'private paddocks' should have access to a shade/shelter, which should be positioned at the gateway (within a surfaced holding yard) and alongside the next 'private paddock', so that two horses can socialise.

Horses in 'private paddocks' should have access to a shade/shelter, which should be positioned at the gateway (within a surfaced holding yard) and alongside the next 'private paddock', so that two horses can socialise.

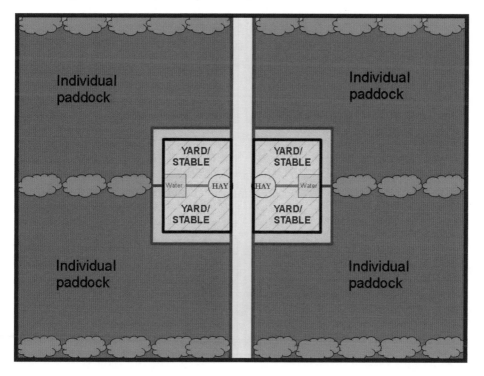

We do not advocate horses socialising over fences, but in this situation, if the partition between the two horses is solid from their chest down (so that they cannot injure a leg) and open above chest height (preferably totally open rather than 'caged'), then two separated horses can and will happily spend many hours 'hanging out' in this area rather than on the sensitive pasture.

When the weather is too wet or too dry the horses can be temporarily prevented from going out of the yard and causing damage that will lead to less quality grazing in the future.

By subdividing any pasture that is available to such horses (as long as this does not create ridiculously small areas) and rotating them around these areas, the land has time to rest and recuperate, resulting in better quality grazing for the horses into the future. For the pasture, any rest is better than none.

See the section *Temporary laneways* for ideas about subdividing smaller/awkward areas of land.

Starting from scratch

If you are in the fortunate position of being able to start a horse facility from scratch, you have much planning to do.

Setting up **The Equicentral System** from scratch should cost less than setting up conventional facilities. Money that would be spent on items such as stables, individual shelters etc. can instead be spent on a surfaced holding yard/s with shelters. Don't forget you can create a surface that can be used for riding/training as well!

—

See the third book in this series *The Equicentral System Series Book 3 – Horse Property Planning and Development* for more information about using a surfaced holding yard as a riding surface, and for information about the total planning of a horse property.

—

Minimising laneways

Depending on the layout of the property, it should be possible to minimise laneway usage, particularly if the internal fences are not yet established.

If you are utilising **The Equicentral System** the horses will be living as a herd, moving *themselves* around the property, only ever having access to one paddock at a time, therefore the paddocks should be arranged so that they lead either directly back to the surfaced holding yard or, if this is not possible (in the case of a long narrow property for example), temporary laneways can be constructed (see the section *Temporary laneways*).

Aim to *minimise* laneways for several reasons:

- Laneways take up space that could otherwise be used as pasture for grazing.
- Laneways concentrate hoof activity to a narrow strip and therefore create land degradation problems such as mud/dust, soil erosion, weeds.
- Laneways are difficult to harrow, mow, weed etc.
- Laneways require more fencing and sometimes require surfacing, therefore extra expense.

Laneways take up space that could otherwise be used as pasture for grazing.

If possible, create a layout for your land that reduces or eliminates the need for laneways. There are several ways that you can do this:

- You may be able to have your paddocks 'fan-out' from the surfaced holding yard so that all paddocks lead directly back to this area without the need for laneways.

- You can utilise 'temporary' laneways so that the land used as a laneway is only used as such when necessary and becomes part of the paddock again when not needed as a laneway (see the section **Temporary laneways**).

Property A has a laneway leading to the far paddock but if possible, lay the property out so that there are minimal or no laneways (property B).

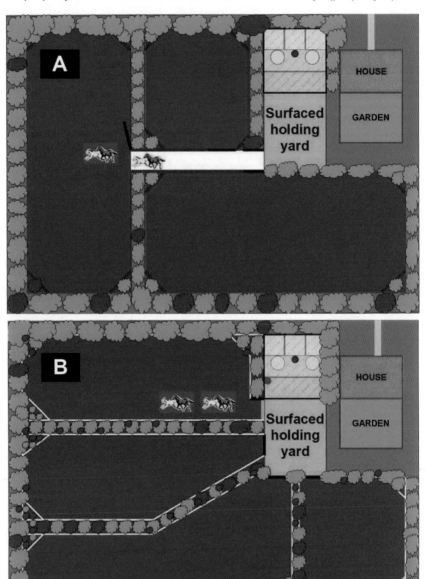

Temporary laneways

A *temporary* laneway can be constructed from temporary electric fence posts (sometimes called 'tread-ins') and electric fence tape to create a 'laneway' that takes the horses to the far end of a long narrow paddock, or even across one paddock to a paddock beyond. This is sometimes preferable to erecting a permanent laneway, because it can be *removed* when the horses are grazing the near section or the near paddock. The land that *would* become a permanent laneway is spared and can be managed as part of the paddock for some of the year; it is far easier to manage land as part of a paddock than to manage land as part of a laneway.

An alternative to using temporary electric fence posts is to put permanent fence posts (e.g. pine poles or steel posts with plastic caps on) in a line where you need them and fasten electric tape carriers to them. This way, an electric tape can be run out through them when necessary and reeled back in when it is not needed.

—

See the third book in this series *The Equicentral System Series Book 3 – Horse Property Planning and Development* for information about fences, including electric fences.

—

A temporary laneway can be used to take horses to a far paddock on a narrow property.

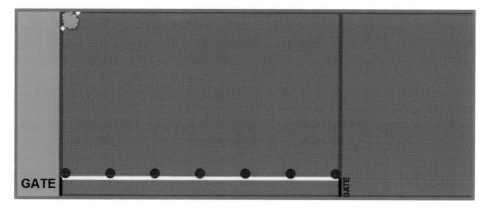

To strip graze a paddock using a temporary laneway, the first stage would look like this....

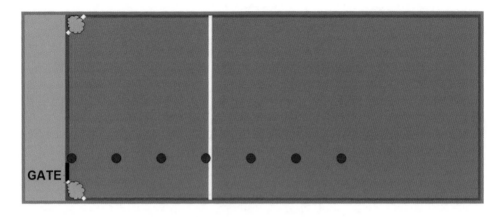

...the second stage would look like this....

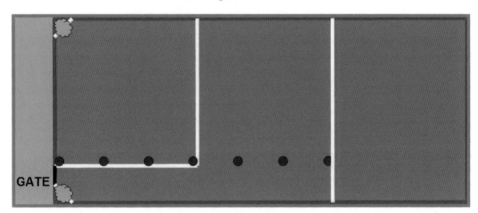

...and the third stage would look like this....

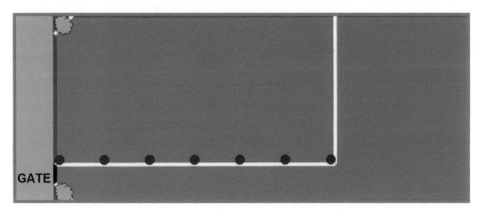

Constructing a holding area

It is imperative that you have a surfaced area for horses to stand. Otherwise, you are quickly going to have mud and dust, soil loss, weeds etc. You are also going to see the skin conditions that are associated with mud such as mud fever/greasy heel etc. If you need to construct a purpose built holding area (rather than utilise something that is already in place) you will need information about this subject.

—

See the third book in this series *The Equicentral System Series Book 3 – Horse Property Planning and Development* for lots more information about constructing a surfaced holding yard.

—

Constructing a shade/shelter

It is imperative that you have shade/shelter for your horse/s. This will increase their need to move themselves back to the holding area and is important for protection both from inclement weather and from insects. There are a huge variety of options ranging from traditional to non-traditional, and from permanent to temporary/relocatable.

—

See the third book in this series *The Equicentral System Series Book 3 – Horse Property Planning and Development* for lots more information about shade/shelters.

—

Fencing considerations

As a general rule, your external (perimeter) fence and any areas in which horses are being confined in a smaller space should have good solid permanent fencing. Anywhere that horses can move away from each other can, if necessary, be fenced inexpensively with electric fencing, certainly initially. Avoid having electric fencing around the holding yard if possible and, if you do use it in laneways, be aware that horses can knock each other into it and it can therefore be stressful for horses when they cannot get out of each other's way.

—

See the third book in this series *The Equicentral System Series Book 3 – Horse Property Planning and Development* for lots more information about fencing.

—

Management solutions

Feeding confined horses

This book does not cover the subject of feeding horses in detail, but this section gives some pointers to keep in mind for confined horses.

The term 'ad-lib' means that something is provided on an 'all you can eat' basis. In the case of hay provision, it means that a horse always has hay available as opposed to being fed measured amounts. It might sound crazy to feed a horse 'ad-lib', but this is what a horse has evolved to deal with. In the naturally-living situation, they are surrounded by their food and graze in bouts and with periods of rest, rather than eating a 'meal' as a predator does and then having to go without food until they make another kill.

In the domestic situation, we can more closely copy this natural situation of having ad-lib feed by aiming to have low energy ad-lib hay or pasture available for our horses.

Horses that are confined, and therefore unable to graze, must be provided with plenty of fibre to make up for not being able to graze. – remember – without fibre, acid builds up in the stomach.

One of the most common (and deadliest) mistakes made by horse owners is to feed their horse as they would feed themselves or their dog - on small but high energy meals. Humans and dogs naturally eat much smaller amounts of higher energy food (relatively). This is because their food types are relatively higher in energy (meat and relatively easy to digest vegetables etc.). Horses are completely different; their food (pasture plants) is difficult and time consuming to digest and therefore, confined horses should be provided with enough hay to allow them to 'graze' as and when they want. As already mentioned, ideally, hay should be provided on an 'ad-lib' (an 'all-you-can-eat') basis when they are not grazing.

Another common horse management mistake is to 'lock horses up' without food in an attempt to reduce their feed intake; this practice is commonly done with horses that are getting fat on pasture. Remember - this is not good horse management because it leads to gorging when the horse is allowed to eat again.

Another common horse management mistake is to 'lock horses up' without food in an attempt to reduce their feed intake; this practice is commonly done with horses that are getting fat on pasture.

If horses have long periods without food, the risks of colic and gastrointestinal ulcers increase and even laminitis can be brought on by the stress caused by incorrect feeding (including 'starving').

Clean but low-energy grass hay is better for feeding horses 'ad-lib'; rather than Lucerne/alfalfa hay, because it is less nutritionally dense. Therefore, more of it can be eaten, thus satisfying the horse's high frequency chewing rates and the guts need to be constantly processing fibre.

If a horse tends to get fat easily, aim to reduce the *energy* value in the hay in order to maintain the quantity hay; for these animals, aim to source hay with a low sugar value. This can be hard to determine, but if you are buying it from a produce/feed store, you need to ask if they have hay that has had a basic nutritional analysis carried out on it (some produce/feed stores will now provide this service). Soaking suspect hay in water (it can then be fed wet) for at least an hour before feeding will help to leach out some of the sugar content.

Be aware that the results of soaking are variable depending on how much sugar there was to start with and the temperature of the water (warm/hot water will leach more sugar). In addition, increase your horse's exercise – this is a very important but often ignored point. Remember - horses are meant to move a lot. It is common for people to go to great lengths to reduce the chance that their horse will develop or have a reoccurrence of laminitis – by 'micro managing' the horse diet. It is particularly surprising that many horse owners will opt to buy expensive supplements and feeds in preference to planning a more naturally active lifestyle for their animals. Increased exercise is a cheaper, more effective way to prevent obesity and it's diseases, it also leads to a mentally more balanced horse. (see the section *Ideas for extra exercise*).

Many people underestimate how much fibre a horse actually needs. An average hay bale (small square) has 10 biscuits (sections) of hay. If a horse is confined for all or most of each day, a medium size (14-15hh) horse needs *at least* 1/3 (3-4 biscuits) of a (heavy compacted) bale to go through its gut daily. A larger horse needs as much as 1/2 of a bale (5 biscuits) or even 3/4 of a bale (7-8 biscuits) of hay per day. This is just a very rough guide, as bales of hay vary very much in weight.

Another rough calculation is that a mature horse needs to eat approximately 2% of its bodyweight in Dry Matter (DM) per day. So a 500kg (1100lb) horse will need 10kg (22lb) of hay (hay does not have much water content so if you are feeding haylage or silage, which does contain water, this figure would be higher). In addition, a horse may need minerals adding to their diet.

These amounts are just to give an inexperienced horse owner a rough idea of the volume a horse actually needs. In reality, a horse should always have access to ad-lib hay when not grazing.

A horse that is working hard may also need supplementary hard feed (e.g. grains or mixes), but be careful as another common mistake that horse owners make is that they tend to overestimate their horse's hard feed requirements.

Remember - horses that are 'group housed' should be able to get out of each other's way and should be separated for supplementary feeding if communal feeding initiates aggression. Horses should ideally be separated into individual yards or stables for the short time that it takes to eat any concentrate feed; both for their own safety and the safety of their handlers.

Changing a horse to 'ad-lib' feeding

If your horse has always had measured/restricted amounts of food rather than ad-lib food then you will have to be careful about changing them over. When horses have been withheld from food they tend to 'gorge' when first allowed to eat at will. Remember - a horse would naturally spend most of its day eating fibre, its whole physiology has evolved to allow it to do this efficiently. When you use restrictive feeding/grazing practices, this is in complete contrast to what the horse has adapted to do and when combined with the horses natural instinct to try to gain weight whenever possible, it is easy to see why many horses develop 'eating disorders'.

So, if the horse is currently living on short stressed grasses (and is overweight), it would *not* be a good idea to switch to turning him or her out on long grasses straightaway; even though these grasses are lower in sugar per mouthful, because the horse in question will initially gorge themselves. **A better strategy would be either of the following:**

Option 1: Over winter – with no access to pasture initially:

- You will need the use of surfaced holding yards – preferably as part of an **Equicentral System.**

- During winter, when the horse is receiving no pasture, feed ad-lib low-energy hay in a surfaced yard – preferably with other horses. You may want to soak this hay in warm water for at least one hour before feeding as a further precaution, particularly if you are not sure what the energy level of that hay is. **An extremely important factor is that the hay does not run out – at all, ever!** This is because, if it does, the horse thinks he or she is being 'starved' again and behaves accordingly (e.g. starts to gorge when food is available again).

- Aim to reduce the horse's weight gradually but significantly over the winter by totally avoiding high energy supplementary feeds, avoiding rugging unless absolutely necessary (but ensure that the horse can get under a shelter) and *increasing exercise* (see the section ***Ideas for extra exercise***). You need to aim for a condition score of no more than 2.5 by the start of spring.

Condition scoring

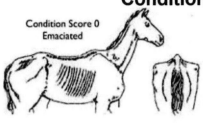

Condition Score 0
Emaciated

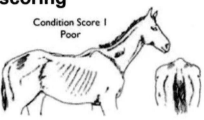

Condition Score I
Poor

Score 0 (Very Poor). *Neck* - marked 'ewe neck' - narrow and slack at base. *Back & ribs* - skin tight over ribs, very prominent backbone. *Pelvis & rump* - very sunken rump, deep cavity under tail, angular pelvis, skin tight.

Score 1 (Poor). *Neck* - 'ewe' shaped, narrow & slack at base. *Back & ribs* - ribs easily visible, skin sunken either side of backbone. *Pelvis & rump* - sunken rump but skin slacker, pelvis and croup highly defined.

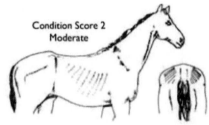

Condition Score 2
Moderate

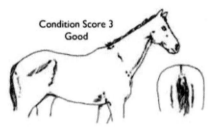

Condition Score 3
Good

Score 2 (Moderate). *Neck* - narrow but firm. *Back & ribs* - ribs just visible, backbone well covered but can be felt. *Pelvis & rump* - flat rump either side of backbone, croup well defined, some fat, slight cavity under tail.

Score 3 (Good). *Neck* - firm, no crest (except in a stallion). *Back & ribs* - ribs just covered but easily felt, no gutter along back, backbone covered but can be felt. *Pelvis & rump* - covered by fat and rounded, no gutter, pelvis easily felt.

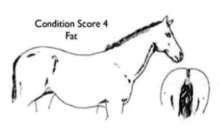

Condition Score 4
Fat

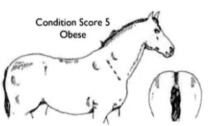

Condition Score 5
Obese

Score 4 (Fat). *Neck* - slight crest. *Back & ribs* - ribs well covered, need firm pressure to feel, gutter along backbone. *Pelvis & rump* - gutter to root of tail, pelvis covered by soft fat - felt only with firm pressure.

Score 5 (Very Fat). *Neck* - marked crest, very wide and firm, lumpy fat. *Back & ribs* - deep gutter along back, back broad and flat, ribs buried cannot be felt. *Pelvis & rump* - deep gutter to root of tail, skin is distended, pelvis buried under fat.

- The horse can still be given minerals etc. if you feel that they are needed, but these do not have to be added to high calorie feed; they can be added to a small amount of chaff.

—

We believe that *not* allowing this naturally occurring weight loss to happen in winter is one of the primary reasons for the obesity epidemic today.

—

- If your land recovers enough to grow pasture before the winter, and this paddock is locked up, you can start to introduce the horse gradually to the pasture over the latter part of the winter. Letting pasture grow long and then allowing horses to harvest it themselves in winter is called 'foggage' or 'standing hay'. This practice has many, many advantages including that it saves the costs of cutting, baling and storing hay (and the risk of it 'failing' as a crop). By mid-winter, it will have more fibre value than nutritional value; in other words, it is ideal for a 'weight challenged' horse.

—

See the second book in this series *The Equicentral System Series Book 2 - Healthy Land, Healthy Pasture, Healthy Horses* for more information about this practice.

—

- When the rest of your land is ready to receive horses again in the spring, you can gradually allow the horse in question to have at first one grazing turnout session (grazing bout) per day over a period of about a week (in addition to ad-lib hay), then allow this session to be longer (for about a week) and so on.
- Extra exercise may be necessary during this period too and it is extremely beneficial if you can do this (see the section *Ideas for extra exercise*).
- By using **The Equicentral System** you will be able to, at first, dictate when that first grazing period takes place; very late evenings (well after sundown) or very early mornings are a good time – but you will need to bring them back in by lunch time at the latest. Initially, avoid allowing the horse to graze between mid-day and nightfall, because this is when the sugars in the grasses are at their highest levels.
- By late spring/early summer, as long as you are keeping a good watch on the horse's body condition score and are not reverting to restricting their low energy hay intake, you should be able to allow night and day grazing bouts with free access to the paddock that is currently in use.
- By the time the pasture is growing higher energy feed in the spring, the horse will have relaxed and will not be as tempted to gorge. If you have carried out the

above steps, the horse will now have a much lower body condition score and will be in a much safer position. You will need to keep up this pattern of reducing the horse's weight every winter and keeping up the extra movement whenever it is necessary.

An extremely important factor is that the hay does not run out – at all, ever!

Option 2 – During summer – with access to pasture.

- This option is if you would like to start changing a horse over to ad-lib feeding right away, without waiting for winter. Again you will need the use of surfaced holding yards – preferably as part of an **Equicentral System**.

- Initially, confine the horse by day, on ad-lib low energy hay. Again, it is imperative that the hay **never** runs out and again, you may want to soak this hay in water before feeding, only allowing one grazing turnout period per day as per the previous example.

- You will need to closely monitor the horse's weight and you should **definitely** increase exercise during this period, which should be easier for you at this time of year (see the section *Ideas for extra exercise*).

- As in the above option, avoid supplementary feeding and rugging. Make sure the horse has access to shade/shelter and they should preferably be kept with other horses. Carry on adding grazing time as per option 1, but **only** if you feel the horse is not increasing weight too fast.

- The idea is that you are initially controlling the horse's intake by allowing ad-lib access to low energy hay, but you are switching the horse over to not feeling restricted *at all*. Remember - restricted feeding can actually increase insulin resistance levels because the body reacts by going into 'starvation mode' - **never lock a horse up without something to eat.**

- Never limit hay, limit grazing time initially if you feel the horse is gaining weight too fast. When winter arrives and for every winter from now on, still aim for the horse to lose some weight, because this is what the horse has done for naturally for eons; lost weight in winter and not been in as dangerous a position when the feed quality increases in the spring. They can then relatively safely gain some weight gradually during spring and summer. This is a better strategy than trying to maintain the horse's weight at exactly the same weight all year round.

- You may need to learn more about pasture plants too, including factors that make them safer, or not as safe, to graze.

Make sure the horse has access to shade/shelter and they should preferably be kept with other horses.

Source - Gina Sykes of Bathurst Equine Agistment - Aus.

Before embarking on any radical changes such as those outlined above, have the horse checked out by an experienced *equine* veterinarian, preferably someone who has a particular interest in the subject of equine obesity. You could also engage an equine nutritionist; preferably an *independent* equine nutritionist.

—

See the second book in this series *The Equicentral System Series Book 2 - Healthy Land, Healthy Pasture, Healthy Horses* for more information.

—

Ideas for extra exercise

Curiously, most pet owners recognise that if they own a dog they should 'walk' it (even if they do not actually do it) but many horse owners do not apply the same ethos to horsekeeping. Maybe because dogs live in or around a home and tend to remind their owners that they want to go out? Horse owners tend to assume that their horse/s get enough exercise if they are tuned out on a pasture but as we now know they usually need more exercise than that, plus they are usually receiving more energy (from pasture/feed) than they are using.

There are various ways, apart from general riding, that you can incorporate *extra* exercise into a horse's management routine.

- Driving - small ponies in particular can be trained to drive. Driving is a good pastime for horses and people.

- Hand walking – there is no reason why you cannot take a horse for a walk, smaller ponies in particular are not difficult to do this with. You could even walk the dog at the same time!

- Running – some owners jog/run with their horse in hand for mutual fitness benefits.

- Hill climbing in hand – if you live in a hilly area you can walk/jog/run the hills and you can use your horse to help you up the hills by holding onto their mane.

- Lunging – just ten minutes a day of trotting on the lunge is great exercise.

- Round penning – like lunging but loose in a round yard.

- 'Riding and leading' – if you are riding anyway, why not lead another horse while doing so?

You (and your horse) may need instruction before carrying out some of these activities, but the benefits will be worth it.

Introducing horses to herd living

Careful introduction of a horse into a herd will vastly reduce any risks and an added bonus is that grazing management is much easier when horses live together, because they can be rotated around areas as a group. One horse per paddock does not allow the pasture any rest and recuperation time; a welfare issue for grass! In fact, 'managing' pasture in this way leads to stressed grass that is not good for horses and land degradation problems.

—

We cover this subject in detail in the second book in this series *The Equicentral System Series Book 2 - Healthy Land, Healthy Pasture, Healthy Horses*.

—

If you decide to integrate your horses into a herd because of the horse welfare *and* land management benefits, there are several things to think about and steps to take so that the integration goes smoothly. First of all, think about each of the horses in question and decide if it will be best to have one herd or more than one herd. To end up with just one herd is the best outcome because this will be much easier for land management, but this may not be possible in your situation.

Some of the factors that will help you to decide include the age and sex of the individual animals; for example, young and boisterous horses may be too energetic for a *very* old horse whereas, older horses, on the other hand are usually very good at holding their own with younger horses up until a certain age (which is different for all horses), when they may start to need more specialised care in general.

It generally works best if there are more mares than geldings in a herd, because some geldings still have some entire (stallion) behaviour and can become protective of mares to the point that they will chase other geldings if mares are present. So, if you decide to have two herds for example, it may be better in this case to have one gelding with the mares in one herd and the rest of the geldings in another herd. This is similar to the natural groups that occur in the naturally-living situation e.g. a stallion with some mares and a bachelor group consisting of males of all ages. All horses are different though and various scenarios can work.

There are many ways that a new horse can be introduced to a group of horses. Remember that the existing group will have a social structure and the introduction of a new member will temporarily disrupt this. It is simply not safe to turn the new member out into the group and 'let them get on with it'. In a confined space, the new horse can be run into or over a fence by the other horses. It is better to let the new horse get to know at least one member of the group in separate, securely fenced yards (preferably 'post and rail') or stables that have an area where two horses can safely interact with each other. This way, the newcomer can approach the fence or wall to greet the other horse, but can also get away if necessary. There will usually be squealing, but this is perfectly normal behaviour when horses meet and greet each other.

It is better to let the new horse get to know at least one member of the group in separate, securely fenced yards (preferably 'post and rail') or stables that have an area where two horses can safely interact with each other.

Once these two horses are accustomed to each other, you can turn them out together and then add other herd members gradually one at a time. Try not to give them any hard feed (if the horses are being supplementary fed), only hay, just before you turn them out so that they get down to grazing sooner. It is safer if the horses are left unshod at least for the initial introductions. Hoof boots can also be used. Make sure that resources are plentiful and easy to reach, for example, situate the water away from a corner so that they can each drink safely and no one gets trapped. The group must be watched very carefully during these times.

Keep in mind that you will usually see the most excitable behaviour between the horses in the first hour or so after turning them out together. It can be challenging when introducing horses to one another for the first time, but as long as it is done in a safe manner, usually after a short, somewhat noisy and lively period things settle down. There is bound to be some initial excitement when two horses meet for the first time, particularly if they have been previously kept alone or are new additions to an established herd. Think about when introducing new cat or dog to an established household, there are normally one of two skirmishes until everyone gets used to each other. This is no different in the horse world, but because they are large, energetic, noisy and valuable animals we are often shocked by the first encounter. We have to be aware that some of that behaviour is horseplay; by its definition in human terms, loud and boisterous, but remember this is what horses do. However, we have to be aware of the difference between play behaviour and aggressive behaviour, and ensure that we monitor the situation. With some horses this can be very difficult, as they have been mentally damaged by the way they have been raised or separated in the past.

The Equicentral System - in conclusion

As we have shown, there are many challenges facing modern horse owners. Traditional systems are not meeting the needs of our modern horses. We have to look at more holistic management systems that can work within the boundaries and limitations of our and that of horse's lifestyles.

The simplest way to achieve this is to accept that although we cannot provide a fully natural lifestyle for our domesticated horses, we can learn from nature and work with it rather than against it. Once we start to do this, everything becomes easier, more productive and healthier. We should also invest time in learning about what our horses actually need, this way we are better equipped to make informed choices not only about how we manage our horses but also in who we turn to for advice when needed.

By becoming more responsible, sustainable and ethical horse owners we can ensure that we strive to create an environment which is conducive to creating healthy land, which then creates healthy pasture to ensure we have healthy horses.

Further reading - A list of our books

Buying a Horse Property

Buying a horse property is probably the most expensive and important purchase you will ever make. Therefore, it is very important that you get it right. There are many factors to consider and there may be compromises that have to be made. This guide to buying a horse property will help you to make many of those very important decisions.

Decisions include factors such as whether to buy developed or undeveloped land? Whether to buy a smaller property nearer the city or a larger property in a rural area? Other factors that you need to think about include the size and layout of the property, the pastures and soil, access to riding areas, the water supply, and any possible future proposals for the area. These subjects and many more are covered in this book.

A useful checklist is also provided so that you can ask the right questions before making this very important decision.

If you are buying a horse property, you cannot afford to miss out on the invaluable information in this book!

The Equicentral System Series Book 1: Horse Ownership Responsible Sustainable Ethical

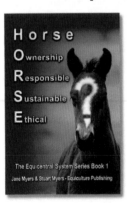

With horse ownership comes great responsibility; we have a responsibility to manage our horses to the best of our ability and to do this sustainably and ethically.

Horse keeping has changed dramatically in the last 30 to 40 years and there are many new challenges facing contemporary horse owners. The modern domestic horse is now much more likely to be kept for leisure purposes than for work and this can have huge implications on the health and well-being of our horses and create heavy demands on our time and resources.

We need to rethink how we keep horses today rather than carry on doing things traditionally simply because that is 'how it has always been done'. We need to look at how we can develop practices that ensure that their needs are met, without compromising their welfare, the environment and our own lifestyle.

This book brings together much of the current research and thinking on responsible, sustainable, ethical horsekeeping so that you can make informed choices when it comes to your own horse management practices. It starts by looking at the way we traditionally keep horses and how this has come about. It then discusses some contemporary issues and offers some solutions in particular a system of horsekeeping that we have developed and call **The Equicentral System.**

For many years now we have been teaching this management system to horse owners in various climates around the world, to great effect. This system has many advantages for the 'lifestyle' of your horse/s, your own lifestyle and for the wider environment - all at the same time, a true win-win situation all round.

The Equicentral System Series Book 2: Healthy Land, Healthy Pasture, Healthy Horses

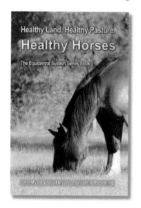

If you watch horses grazing pasture, you would think that they were made for each other. You would in fact be correct; millions of years of evolution have created a symbiotic relationship between equines (and other grazing animals) and grasslands. Our aim as horse owners and as custodians of the land should be to replicate that relationship on our land as closely as possible.

In an ideal world, most horse owners would like to have healthy nutritious pastures on which to graze their horses all year round. Unfortunately, the reality for many horse owners is far from ideal. However, armed with a little knowledge it is usually possible to make a few simple changes in your management system to create an environment which produces healthy, horse friendly pasture, which in turn leads to healthy 'happy' horses.

Correct management of manure, water and vegetation on a horse property is also essential to the well-being of your family, your animals, your property and the wider environment.

This book will help to convince you that good land management is worthwhile on many levels and yields many rewards. You will learn how to manage your land in a way that will save you time and money, keep your horses healthy and content *and* be good for the environment all at the same time. It is one of those rare win-win situations.

The Equicentral System Series Book 3: Horse Property Planning and Development

It does not matter if you are buying an established horse property, starting with a blank canvas or modifying a property you already own; a little forward planning can ensure that your dream becomes your property. Design plays a very important role in all our lives. Good design leads to better living and working spaces and it is therefore very important that we look at our property as a whole with a view to creating a design that will work for our chosen lifestyle, our chosen horse pursuit, keep our horses healthy and happy, enhance the environment and to be pleasing to the eye, all at the same time.

Building horse facilities is an expensive operation. Therefore, planning what you are going to have built, or build yourself is an important first step. Time spent in the planning stage will help to save time and money later on.

The correct positioning of fences, laneways, buildings, yards and other horse facilities is essential for the successful operation and management of a horse property and can have great benefits for the environment. If it is well planned, the property will be a safer, more productive, more enjoyable place to work and spend time with horses. At the same time, it will be labour saving and cost effective due to improved efficiency, as well as more aesthetically pleasing, therefore it will be a more valuable piece of real estate. If the property is also a commercial enterprise, then a well-planned property will be a boon to your business. This book will help you make decisions about what you need, and where you need it; it could save you thousands.

Horse Properties - A Management Guide

This book is an overview of how you can successfully manage a horse property - sustainably and efficiently. It also complements our one day workshop - *Healthy Land, Healthy Pasture, Healthy Horses*.

This book offers many practical solutions for common problems that occur when managing a horse property. It also includes the management system that we have designed, called - **The Equicentral System**.

This book is a great introduction to the subject of land management for horse-keepers. It is packed with pictures and explanations that help you to learn, and will make you want to learn even more.

Some of the subjects included in this book are:
The grazing behaviour of horses.
The paddock behaviour of horses.
The dunging behaviour of horses.
Integrating horses into a herd.
Land degradation problems.
The many benefits of pasture plants.
Horses and biodiversity.
Grasses for horses.
Simple solutions for bare soil.
Grazing and pasture management.
Grazing systems.
Condition scoring.
Manure management... and much more!

Horse Rider's Mechanic Workbook 1: Your Position

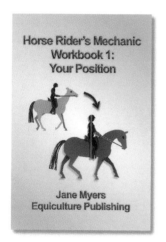

Many common horse riding problems, including pain and discomfort when riding, can be attributed to poor rider position. Often riders are not even aware of what is happening to various parts of their body when they are riding. Improving your position is the key to improving your riding. It is of key importance because without addressing the fundamental issues, you cannot obtain an 'independent seat'.

This book looks at each part of your body in great detail, starting with your feet and working upwards through your ankles, knees and hips. It then looks at your torso, arms, hands and head. Each chapter details what each of these parts of your body should be doing and what you can do to fix any problems you have with them. It is a step by step guide which allows you to fix your own position problems.

After reading this book, you will have a greater understanding of what is happening to the various parts of your body when you ride and why. You will then be able to continue to improve your position, your seat and your riding in general. This book also provides instructors, riding coaches and trainers with lots of valuable rider position tips for teaching clients. You cannot afford to miss out on this great opportunity to learn!

Horse Rider's Mechanic Workbook 2: Your Balance

Horse Rider's Mechanic
Workbook 2:
Your Balance

Jane Myers
Equiculture Publishing

Without good balance, you cannot ride to the best of your ability. After improving your position (the subject of the first book in this series), improving your balance will lead to you becoming a more secure and therefore confident rider. Improving your balance is the key to *further* improving your riding. Most riders need help with this area of their riding life, yet it is not a commonly taught subject.

This book contains several lessons for each of the three paces, walk, trot and canter. It builds on **Horse Rider's Mechanic Workbook 1: Your Position**, teaching you how to implement your now improved position and become a safer and more secure rider.

The lessons allow you to improve at your own pace, in your own time. They will compliment any instruction you are currently receiving because they concentrate on issues that are generally not covered by most instructors.

This book also provides instructors, riding coaches and trainers with lots of valuable tips for teaching clients how to improve their balance. You cannot afford to miss out on this great opportunity to learn!

You can read the beginning of each of these books (for free) on the on the Equiculture website www.equiculture.com.au

We also have a website just for Horse Riders Mechanic www.horseridersmechanic.com

Most of our books are available in various formats including paperback, as a PDF download and as a Kindle ebook. You can find out more on our websites where we offer fantastic package deals for our books!

Make sure you sign up for our mailing list while you are on our websites so that you find out when they are published. You will also be able to find out about our workshops and clinics while on the websites.

Recommended websites and books

Our websites www.equiculture.com.au and www.horseridersmechanic.com have extensive information about horsekeeping, horse care and welfare, riding and training. Please visit them and you will find links to other informative websites and books.

Bibliography of scientific papers

Please go to our website www.equiculture.com.au for a list of scientific publications that were used for this book and our other books.

Final thoughts

Thank you for reading this book. We sincerely hope that you have enjoyed it. Please consider leaving a review of this book at the place you bought it from, or contacting us with feedback, stuart@equiculture.com.au so that others may benefit from your reading experience.

Made in the USA
Lexington, KY
11 August 2016